Childhood
Obsessive
Compulsive
Disorder

Developmental Clinical Psychology and Psychiatry Series

Series Editor: Alan E. Kazdin, Yale University

Recent volumes in this series . . .

Childhood Obsessive Compulsive Disorder

Greta Francis
Rod A. Gragg

Volume 35
Developmental Clinical Psychology and Psychiatry

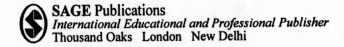

SAGE Publications
International Educational and Professional Publisher
Thousand Oaks   London   New Delhi

For information address:

SAGE Publications, Inc.
2455 Teller Road
Thousand Oaks, California 91320
E-mail: order@sagepub.com

SAGE Publications Ltd.
6 Bonhill Street
London EC2A 4PU
United Kingdom

SAGE Publications India Pvt. Ltd.
M-32 Market
Greater Kailash I
New Delhi 110 048 India

Printed in the United States of America

Library of Congress Cataloging-in-Publication Data

Francis, Greta.
    Childhood obsessive compulsive disorder / Greta Francis and Rod A.
Gragg.
        p.   cm.—(Developmental clinical psychology and psychiatry;
v. 35)
    Includes bibliographical references and index.
    ISBN 0-8039-5921-4 (cloth: alk. paper).—ISBN 0-8039-5922-2 (pbk.: alk.
paper)
    1. Obsessive-compulsive disorder in children.   I. Gragg, Rod A.
II. Title.   III. Series.
RJ506.O25F73   1996
618.92'85227—dc20
                                                                        96-10084

This book is printed on acid-free paper.

96 97 98 99 00 01 10 9 8 7 6 5 4 3 2 1

Sage Production Editor: Michèle Lingre
Sage Typesetter: Andrea D. Swanson

CONTENTS

SERIES EDITOR'S INTRODUCTION

Interest in child development and adjustment is by no means new. Yet only recently has the study of children benefited from advances in both clinical and scientific research. Advances in the social and biological sciences, the emergence of disciplines and subdisciplines that focus exclusively on childhood and adolescence, and greater appreciation of the impact of influences such as the family, peers, and school have helped accelerate research on developmental psychopathology. Apart from interest in the study of child development and adjustment for its own sake, the need to address clinical problems of adulthood naturally draws one to investigate precursors in childhood and adolescence.

Within a relatively brief period, the study of psychopathology among children and adolescents has proliferated considerably. Several different professional journals, annual book series, and handbooks devoted entirely to the study of children and adolescents and their adjustment document the proliferation of work in the field. Nevertheless, there is a paucity of resource material that presents information in an authoritative, systematic, and disseminable fashion. There is a need within the field to convey the latest developments and to represent different disciplines, approaches, and conceptual views to the topics of childhood and adolescent adjustment and maladjustment.

The Sage Series on **Developmental Clinical Psychology and Psychiatry** is designed to uniquely serve several needs of the field. The series encompasses individual monographs prepared by experts in the fields of clinical child psychology, child psychiatry, child development, and related disciplines. The primary focus is on *developmental psychopathology*, which refers broadly here to the diagnosis, assessment, treatment, and prevention of problems that arise in the period from infancy through adolescence. A working assumption of the series is that

vii

understanding, identifying, and treating problems of youth must draw on multiple disciplines and diverse views within a given discipline.

The task for individual contributors is to present the latest theory and research on various topics, including specific types of dysfunction, diagnostic and treatment approaches, and special problem areas that affect adjustment. Core topics within clinical work are addressed by the series. Authors are asked to bridge potential theory, research, and clinical practice and to outline the current status and future directions. The goals of the series and the tasks presented to individual contributors are demanding. We have been extremely fortunate in recruiting leaders in the fields who have been able to translate their recognized scholarship and expertise into highly readable works on contemporary topics.

The present book focuses on childhood obsessive-compulsive disorder. Dr. Greta Francis and Dr. Rod A. Gragg present the latest in theory, research, and practice. The book presents diagnostic, epidemiological, and etiological factors of the disorder and its many variations. Assessment methods and their utility in research and practice are carefully documented. The various forms of psychosocial and biological treatments are also examined. Detailed case examples are provided to convey the complexities of the disorders, the scope of impairment with which they may be associated, and what can be done to intervene. There are very special features of this book: The research is current, authoritative, and incisively presented. In addition, there is no neglect of clinical issues and application. Apart from detailed case studies, the book provides appendixes that include measures of obsessive-compulsive disorder and a manual for one of the treatments (cognitive behavioral treatment) that can be used. The ease with which the authors move from theory, research, and practice makes this a rather unique contribution to the literature in developmental psychopathology. We are quite fortunate to have this as a part of the series.

Alan E. Kazdin, PhD

1

CLINICAL PRESENTATION

This chapter begins with a description of the diagnostic features of Obsessive-Compulsive Disorder (OCD), including case examples of how symptoms may present in children and adolescents. A concise overview of etiological theories is then provided, followed by information regarding the epidemiology of childhood OCD. This chapter concludes with a discussion of differential diagnosis and comorbidity.

DIAGNOSIS

The most recent version of the *Diagnostic and Statistical Manual for Mental Disorders (DSM-IV*; American Psychiatric Association [APA], 1994) defines the essential features of OCD as recurrent obsessions or compulsions that are time-consuming (take more than 1 hour per day), interfere significantly with the person's functioning, or cause distress. In addition, recognition that these symptoms are excessive or unreasonable is required for adults but not for children. The content of the OCD symptoms is not limited to another psychiatric diagnosis (e.g., preoccupation with hair pulling in Trichotillomania), and the problems are not due to the direct physiological effects of a substance (e.g., drugs) or a medical problem.

Obsessions

The *DSM-IV* defines *obsessions* as recurrent thoughts, images, or impulses that are anxiety-provoking and are perceived as intrusive or senseless. The person makes attempts to ignore or suppress the obsessive thoughts, often without success. At times, an individual will attempt to neutralize obsessions by engaging in compulsive behaviors. The person recognizes that the obsessive thoughts are products of his or her own mind (in contrast to thought insertion experienced by individuals with psychotic symptoms). Obsessions are not merely worries about everyday or real-life problems (e.g., worrying about final exams or the actual illness of a family member). Youngsters with OCD may have difficulty describing the specific content of their obsessions. They often report that their rituals are driven by thoughts that "something isn't right" or that "something bad will happen" if they do not perform the rituals. When youth are able to identify the specific content of their thoughts, obsessions typically fall within the seven major categories described next.

Contamination Obsessions. Contamination obsessions typically involve excessive concerns about germs, disease, and cleanliness. Young children are likely to report general worries about people or objects being "germy" or "icky." A child may become extremely upset and fearful of getting germs after observing his "sweaty" father touch dishes, silverware, or food in the kitchen. Older children and adolescents may voice fears of contracting specific illnesses. This was the case for a girl who presented for treatment in our clinic due to her extreme fear of getting AIDS. As is common in youngsters with contamination obsessions, she was hypervigilant to the appearance of her surroundings. She believed that slight discolorations on the sidewalk in front of the hospital and minor blemishes on chairs in the waiting room were actually blood stains that would provide an avenue for transmission of the HIV virus.

Somatic Obsessions. Somatic obsessions are persistent, repetitive thoughts about physical concerns. Children may experience intrusive thoughts that they have a tumor or that they are developing sensory impairments. Often, these thoughts are prompted by routine life events, such as having a headache or watching a television show about someone with a disability. One youngster in our clinic became panic-stricken after he moved from a well-lit to a darkened room in which he could not see. The boy was convinced that this event indicated that he was losing his sight permanently, and he began having the recurrent intrusive thought, "I'm going blind."

Sexual/Aggressive Obsessions. These obsessions typically involve recurrent thoughts or images that one has committed an unacceptable sexual or aggressive thought or act in the past or is likely to do so in the future. Children and adolescents may experience intrusive images of masturbating in front of their teacher or thoughts of killing their parents or siblings. Such images and thoughts often are associated with extreme distress and feelings of guilt.

Need for Symmetry and Exactness. These obsessions are characterized by excessive concern about putting objects in a specific position, scheduling events in a certain order, doing and undoing motor acts in an exact fashion, or making sure that things are precisely symmetrical. For example, a young girl might worry at school about whether her dolls and stuffed animals are lined up on her bed precisely as she left them in the morning. Often, the youngster fears a disastrous consequence if things are not "just right." This was the case with an adolescent male from our clinic who worried that something bad would happen unless he walked out of a room exactly the same way he walked into it initially.

Hoarding Obsessions. Youth with hoarding obsessions often worry that things should not be thrown away just in case they might be needed later. They may think that a catastrophic consequence will result if they fail to keep an item. In one case, an adolescent with whom we worked described an intense fear that he would die unless he picked up and saved any leaves and rocks that he came upon in his travels. Another boy catastrophized about the consequences of throwing away small pieces of paper that he stored in his bedroom. He worried that he would fail his exams, not graduate from high school, be denied entrance into college, and never secure a job.

Doubting Obsessions. The cardinal feature of doubting obsessions is incessant worrying that one will be responsible for a terrible consequence resulting from one's failure to fulfill an obligation or complete a task correctly. One youngster spent hours worrying about whether or not he remembered to schedule his next therapy appointment. Another child had intrusive thoughts that he might have forgotten to unplug the television in his room and feared that he would be responsible for causing an electrical fire.

Religious Obsessions. Religious obsessions typically involve thoughts about committing or having committed an immoral act or sin. Excessive guilt and fear of going to hell are often present. One adolescent boy began performing rituals to "make amends" for having broken an earlier "promise to God." While attempting to lose weight, he had promised that he would refrain from eating candy. When he later ate a candy bar, he experienced extreme guilt and vowed that he would always do things "the right way" in the future. While in the midst of routine activities, he began experiencing the intrusive thought, "this is a sin." This caused him immediately to stop whatever he was doing or saying to determine how God would want him to behave. For example, on one occasion, he experienced the intrusive thought when he happened to be scratching his eyebrow with his finger. He then scratched his eyebrow with the collar of his shirt in an attempt to "undo the sin." Still feeling uncomfortable, he became confused about which of these methods was the right way to scratch his eyebrow and went back and forth between the two until his anxiety decreased. Religious obsessions also may occur in response to thoughts or behaviors that are a normal part of adolescent development. For example, an adolescent girl seen in our clinic frequently had intrusive thoughts that she would go to hell because of her sexual thoughts about her boyfriend.

Compulsions

The *DSM-IV* defines *compulsions* as repeated behaviors or mental acts that a person feels compelled or driven to perform, either in response to an obsession or according to a self-imposed, rigidly applied rule. Typically, compulsions are irrational and maladaptive behaviors performed in an attempt to reduce distress, to prevent a perceived catastrophic outcome, or to neutralize an obsession. The six major types of compulsions are described next.

Washing and Cleaning Compulsions. These rituals typically involve excessive washing and cleaning of oneself and one's surroundings, as well as active avoidance of objects, places, or persons considered to be unclean. They usually are associated with contamination obsessions and can present in a variety of ways, as illustrated by the following case examples. One 7-year-old boy who was evaluated in our outpatient clinic washed his hands repeatedly to the point of causing significant chapping and bleeding. Before going to school in the morning, he rubbed liquid soap onto his hands and around his nose to prevent "catching germs." In addition, he avoided all contact with his younger brother, whom he considered "germy." Another child required her mother to do her laundry every day to make sure that her dirty clothes did not contaminate the rest of her belongings. An 8-year-old boy closely examined packages of food that his mother brought home from the grocery store and refused to eat anything from a package that was even slightly bent for fear that "poison" was in the food.

Checking Compulsions. Youngsters with these rituals typically feel an overwhelming urge to check and recheck objects and/or actions. This is often done in an attempt to alleviate anxiety associated with obsessions involving doubt or the need for symmetry and exactness. For example, a boy who feared being responsible for causing a fire repeatedly checked the position of furniture in his bedroom to ensure that nothing was close to an electrical outlet. A 10-year-old girl repeatedly checked the faucets, the position of the shower curtain, and the light switches in a bathroom at home. She also could not sleep until she had repeatedly checked a variety of locks inside and outside her house (e.g., the gate of the swimming pool in her backyard, the back door, the basement door). She felt compelled to perform these rituals until she felt "just right." A high school student repeatedly telephoned the clinic to make sure he had scheduled his next therapy appointment. While driving to his appointments, he would often retrace his route to check the road for dead bodies of pedestrians he believed he had run over. Finally, a child who arranged her barrettes in two precise rows, sorted by color, was late for school every morning because she could not leave her house without repeatedly checking the position of the barrettes on her dresser.

Repeating Compulsions. These rituals involve redoing physical or mental acts a certain number of times or until it feels just right. We have evaluated a number of children with repeating rituals. One boy needed to turn light switches on and off, get up and down from a seated position, and retrace his steps when walking through rooms until it felt right. Another child felt the urge to touch the doorknob with her left hand whenever she did so with her right hand. An adolescent boy had to rethink the phrase "I did not cheat" 10 times in response to an obsessive thought that he had looked at the test paper of another student. As commonly seen in childhood OCD, repeated requests for reassurance from parents were exhibited by an 11-year-old boy who constantly asked whether he was going blind, might vomit at school, or was going to die.

Counting Compulsions. Children with these rituals often have special or lucky numbers that dictate the number of times they must do, say, or think things. One 13-year-old girl identified two and five as her lucky numbers. She insisted on wearing two pairs of underwear at once, counting to five while turning faucets on and off, and repeating everything she said twice. An older adolescent girl avoided writing three, seven, or nine words on a line and using the third, seventh, or ninth line on a piece of paper. She also avoided looking at digital clocks whenever these numbers were displayed.

Ordering Compulsions. Ordering compulsions are typically associated with obsessions involving the need for symmetry and exactness. It is common for children with these rituals to arrange their belongings in a certain order or to abide by rigid schedules. For example, one young boy arranged his stuffed animals in a precise fashion on his bed and placed his clothes on color-coded hangers in the closet. An adolescent girl developed a rigid schedule in which various activities were performed at fixed times throughout the day. There were five children in her neighborhood with whom she wished to visit. Thus, she divided her afternoons into five time blocks, allowing 48 minutes to visit each child. In the event that one of these neighbors was not at home, she returned to sit in her backyard (with an alarm clock) and waited until the time of her next scheduled visit. Another adolescent engaged in a mental ritual in which he went through a list in his head of all the people he knew and ordered them from those he liked least to those he liked most.

Hoarding Compulsions. These rituals, which often occur in response to hoarding obsessions, involve the inability to throw things away or the need to collect useless objects. For example, an adolescent boy was unable to throw away any piece of paper in his bedroom for fear that he would lose important study material needed for school tests. Another adolescent collected pieces of trash (e.g., drinking straw wrappers, gum wrappers, soda can rings, strings that she found on her clothing), which were kept in large plastic bags in her bedroom. She was unable to stop this behavior even when it became difficult for her to maneuver through the room due to the accumulation of trash.

Symptom Presentation

Obsessive-compulsive symptoms in children and adolescents closely resemble those found in adults with OCD (Rapoport, Swedo, & Leonard, 1992). The types and frequencies of obsessive-compulsive symptoms also have been found to be consistent across different cultures (Allsopp & Verduyn, 1990; Honjo et al., 1989; Thomsen, 1991). The most common obsessive thoughts reported by youngsters with OCD are concerns about germs and contamination, and the most common rituals involve washing and cleaning (Allsopp & Verduyn, 1990; Honjo et al., 1989; Thomsen, 1991). The general types of obsessive-compulsive symptoms have remained essentially the same since first described in the early 1900s; however, the specific content of symptoms may be influenced by historical events. For example, a focus of contamination fears in the 1920s was syphilis, whereas recent reports have described fear of AIDS in children with OCD (Fisman & Walsh, 1994; Wagner & Sullivan, 1991). It is typical for children to present with both obsessions and compulsions, although a minority report only one or the other (Thomsen, 1991). Furthermore, most youngsters present with a variety of different obsessions and compulsions (Hanna, 1995; Rettew, Swedo, Leonard, Lenane, & Rapoport, 1992), and the specific types of symptoms are likely to change over time. Rettew et al. (1992) studied 79 children and adolescents with OCD over approximately a 4-year period and found that none of them maintained the same symptom constellation from baseline to follow-up. However, no discernible patterns of change in symptom presentation were observed.

ETIOLOGY

Several theories have been proposed to explain the etiology of OCD. Both biological and psychological mechanisms have been postulated as causal factors. Biological models have implicated brain structure and function, neurochemistry, and genetic factors in the development of OCD. Psychological models have been based on psychodynamic, learning, and family systems theories.

Biological Models

Brain Structure and Function. Sallee and Greenawald (1995) reviewed the literature on the neurobiology of OCD. Studies that have examined the brain structures of adults with childhood-onset OCD using neuroimaging techniques, such as magnetic resonance imagery (MRI) and X-ray computed tomography (CT), have failed to find overt structural abnormalities. Assessments of brain functioning in this population have produced mixed results. Electrophysiological studies using electroencephalogram (EEG) and evoked potential recordings have found no specific abnormalities in children and adolescents, although abnormalities have been noted in adults with OCD. Positron emission tomography (PET scan) studies have found hypermetabolism in certain areas of the brain (e.g., the orbital frontal cortex) in adults with OCD; and some studies have documented changes in brain metabolism after successful behavioral and/or pharmacological treatment of OCD symptoms (Baxter et al., 1992; Benkelfat et al., 1990; Swedo, Leonard, et al., 1992; Swedo, Pietrini, et al., 1992). OCD may be related to basal ganglia dysfunction, as suggested by the high prevalence of obsessive-compulsive symptoms in children and adolescents with Sydenham's Chorea, a neurological disorder characterized by involuntary jerky movements of the extremities thought to be caused by disease of the basal ganglia (Swedo et al., 1993; Swedo, Rapoport, Cheslow, et al., 1989). Finally, neuropsychological testing completed on adolescents with OCD has revealed deficits suggestive of abnormalities in the frontal and caudate regions of the brain.

Neurochemistry. It has been hypothesized that there is a relationship between OCD and the neurotransmitter serotonin. Support for this theory is based primarily on evidence that OCD symptoms decrease in response to treatment with medications that affect serotonin levels. For example, Flament, Rapoport, Murphy, Berg, and Lake (1987) reported that treatment with clomipramine (a serotonergic agent) resulted in reduced symptoms and altered blood levels of serotonin in children and adolescents with OCD.

Genetic Factors. There are a small number of studies examining the role of genetic factors in OCD. Higher concordance rates for OCD have been found in identical twins (approximately 65%) compared with fraternal twins (approximately 15%) (see Pauls, Raymond, & Robertson, 1991; Steketee, 1993). In addition, increased rates of OCD symptoms have been reported in first-degree relatives of individuals with OCD (Clark & Bolton, 1985b; Lenane et al., 1990).

Psychological Models

Psychodynamic Theory. Pitman (1991) summarized the psychodynamic conceptualization of the roots of OCD. According to this theory,

obsessional neurosis results from fixation at the anal stage of development or regression to this stage resulting from frustration at a higher
developmental level. The anal stage is hypothesized to be associated
with rigidity and overcontrol. These characteristics manifest themselves
as obsessive-compulsive symptoms. Although it has been suggested
that negative experiences with toilet training during the anal stage may
be associated with the development of OCD, empirical studies have
failed to document such a relationship (e.g., Judd, 1965).

Learning Theory. Mowrer's (1960) two-factor theory explains the
development and maintenance of fear responses as resulting from classical
and operant conditioning, respectively. It is hypothesized that previously
neutral thoughts become anxiety provoking when they are inadvertently
paired with aversive stimuli. For example, if a man were having sexual
thoughts while plugging in his power drill and received a sudden electrical
shock, he would experience anxiety associated with sexual thoughts in the
future. The maintenance of rituals and avoidance behaviors is explained by
the principle of negative reinforcement. That is, the performance of these
behaviors results in anxiety reduction, increasing the likelihood that they
will be repeated. The man mentioned earlier might develop checking rituals
to ensure that he and his possessions are not near electrical outlets. He is
likely to continue his checking rituals because he "feels better" after doing
them. Although there is substantial evidence to support the notion that
obsessive-compulsive symptoms are maintained via operant learning, the
role of classical conditioning in the development of symptoms generally
has not been substantiated (see Steketee, 1993).

Family Systems Theory. Systems theorists view obsessive-compulsive
symptoms in children and adolescents, along with other forms of psychopathology, as resulting from problematic family interactions (Haley,
1977; Minuchin & Fishman, 1981). Symptoms in the identified patient
serve a protective function by enabling the family to maintain its dysfunc-
tional organizational patterns (e.g., poor boundaries, weak parental coali-
tions). For example, a young girl's washing rituals would maintain balance
within a family by allowing parents to come together to focus on the
problematic behavior of their daughter rather than deal with unresolved
marital conflicts. Systems theory does not offer an explanation for why
OCD develops rather than other symptoms that could serve the same
function for the family. Furthermore, the applicability of family systems
theory to the etiology of OCD has not been empirically evaluated.

Although the exact causes of OCD remain a mystery, a review of the available literature suggests that certain individuals may have a biological predisposition to develop OCD. However, the factors influencing the eventual manifestation of symptoms in those at biological risk for developing the disorder are still not clear. Even so, there is evidence implicating negative reinforcement as the mechanism by which symptoms are maintained. Clearly, further research is necessary before definitive conclusions can be made about the etiology of OCD.

EPIDEMIOLOGY

Prevalence

The Epidemiological Catchment Area (ECA) Survey estimated the prevalence of psychiatric diagnoses in five community samples of adults (Karno, Golding, Sorensen, & Burnam, 1988). According to this survey, 2.5% plus or minus (+/−) 0.2% of the population were diagnosed with OCD currently or in the past (lifetime prevalence). Approximately 1.2% +/− 0.1% of these adults had current OCD diagnoses (point prevalence). Prevalence rates did not differ for males and females after the investigators controlled for other demographic variables (e.g., age, marital status, employment status, ethnicity).

The prevalence of OCD in youth has been assessed in community samples in the United States, Israel, and Denmark. Flament et al. (1988) surveyed 4,551 9th to 12th grade students in a semirural county in the United States. Participants initially completed a self-report screening instrument that assessed the presence of OCD symptoms. Those students with high scores on this measure then participated in a structured diagnostic interview to confirm a diagnosis of OCD. Results indicated a lifetime prevalence of 1.9% +/− 0.7% and a point prevalence of 1.0% +/− 0.5%. In a study of 562 16- to 17-year-old inductees into the Israeli army, the point prevalence of OCD diagnosis was estimated to be 3.6% +/− 0.7% of the sample (Zohar et al., 1992). Given that all youth in Israel are required to serve in the military, this sample is believed to be representative of the entire population of 16- to 17-year-olds. Finally, Thomsen (1993) found the prevalence of significant self-reported obsessive-compulsive symptoms to range from 4.1% to 10% of 1,032 11- to 17-year-old school children in Denmark. In these three studies of youngsters from community samples, the gender ratio for OCD was found to be roughly equivalent. There is no current information available regarding the prevalence or gender ratio of

OCD in community samples of children under the age of 11. It is important to keep in mind that estimates based on community samples may underestimate the true prevalence of OCD in children and adolescents because those with severe or disabling symptomatology may not be included in the sample pool (e.g., children unable to attend school). Furthermore, the prevalence of OCD in youth would be expected to be lower than that found in adults, given that children have not yet passed through the age period of highest risk for development of the disorder.

Estimates of the prevalence of OCD in clinical samples have been conducted using retrospective chart reviews of psychiatrically treated children and adolescents. In the United States, estimates of the prevalence of OCD among inpatient and outpatient clinical populations have ranged from 0.2% to 1.2% (Hollingsworth, Tanguay, Grossman, & Pabst, 1980; Judd, 1965). Prevalence has been estimated to be higher in clinical samples of Danish (1.33%) and Japanese (5.0%) youth (Honjo et al., 1989; Thomsen & Mikkelsen, 1991). Of children and adolescents who presented with anxiety disorders in an outpatient clinic in the United States, 14.9% had a lifetime prevalence of OCD (Last, Perrin, Hersen, & Kazdin, 1992). Overall, there is a preponderance of males among children referred for treatment of OCD (Hanna, 1995; Hollingsworth et al., 1980; Honjo et al., 1989; Swedo, Rapoport, Leonard, Lenane, & Cheslow, 1989; Thomsen, 1991). Given that only 25% of youth with OCD are likely to seek treatment from a mental health professional, prevalence rates based on clinical populations also may underestimate the number of children and adolescents with OCD (Whitaker et al., 1990).

Onset of Symptoms

Age of Onset. OCD generally begins in late adolescence or early adulthood (Rachman, 1985), with 65% of patients developing the disorder before age 25 (Rasmussen & Tsuang, 1986). Flament et al. (1988) reported the average age of onset of OCD to be 12.8 years in their community sample of high school students. In clinical samples of youth with OCD, the average age of onset has ranged from 7.5 to 11.6 years, with the disorder found in children as young as 3 years of age (Hollingsworth et al., 1980; Honjo et al., 1989; Judd, 1965; Last et al., 1992; Thomsen & Mikkelsen, 1991).

Onset Pattern. Typically, the onset pattern of OCD is gradual. Hanna (1995) found that 55% of a sample of 31 children and adolescents with OCD had an insidious onset over a period of years and that 39%

reported a gradual onset over a period of weeks to months. A minority of youngsters (6%) presented with a sudden and acute onset of symptoms over a period of days. Many children with OCD are symptomatic for years prior to presenting for mental health treatment (Allsopp & Verduyn, 1990; Rettew et al., 1992).

Precipitating Events. A significant proportion of children and family members identify a precipitant, although not causal, event to the onset or worsening of OCD symptoms. Rettew et al. (1992) found that 38% of 79 youngsters with OCD believed that common incidents such as moving, media events, and minor physical illnesses were associated with the onset of symptoms. Interestingly, only one case involved an actual traumatic event (i.e., the child's mattress caught fire from an electric blanket). Although one might logically assume that this event would have led to the development of checking rituals, the child's OCD symptoms actually involved washing compulsions in this case.

Prognosis

In untreated adults with OCD, the course is typically chronic and deteriorating, although periodic remissions may occur (APA, 1994; Turner & Beidel, 1988). Despite the negative outcomes that have been associated with OCD, Stanley (1992) noted that approximately 70% of adults are able to be treated successfully using behavior therapy techniques (i.e., exposure and response prevention). Although little research has evaluated the prognosis of youth with untreated OCD, Berg et al. (1989) conducted a 2-year prospective follow-up study of a largely untreated community sample of adolescents who had been diagnosed with OCD-spectrum disorders. They reported that 50% of subjects diagnosed as having lifetime or current OCD at the initial interview obtained the same diagnosis at the 2-year follow-up, and 81% were given a lifetime diagnosis of either OCD or subclinical OCD at the follow-up interview. The authors concluded that a diagnosis of OCD in adolescence, as in adulthood, is indicative of a serious disorder that is associated with ongoing psychopathology. In addition to persistent obsessive-compulsive symptoms, youth who have been diagnosed with OCD may be at increased risk for the development of other anxiety or mood disorders and Avoidant Personality Disorder in adulthood when compared with normal and psychiatric controls, respectively (Flament et al., 1990; Thomsen & Mikkelsen, 1993). Although there is limited

TABLE 1.1 Normal Developmental Rituals and Superstitions

Age	Normal Developmental Rituals
2.5 years	Rigid routines around eating, bathing, and bedtime
3 to 5 years	Repetitive themes during solitary play activities (e.g., building a tower of blocks and knocking it down repeatedly)
5 to 6 years	Elaborate rules and rhymes associated with group games (e.g., jump rope, hopscotch)
6 to 11 years	Superstitious games (e.g., crossing one's fingers when telling a lie, using "super cootie protection" to prevent "cootie" contamination); commonly accepted collections (e.g., coins, baseball cards, stamps)
12 years and older	Preoccupation with popular activities or famous people (e.g., playing Sega, becoming infatuated with television stars); superstitious rituals related to competitive sports (e.g., praying in the locker room before a game, maintaining a routine associated with a streak of good luck)

information available regarding long-term outcomes of children and adolescents who have been treated for OCD, preliminary findings suggest that the prognosis may improve after behavioral and pharmacological treatments (for reviews see Allen, Leonard, & Swedo, 1995; March, 1995).

DIFFERENTIAL DIAGNOSIS

When a child presents with recurrent thoughts or ritualistic behaviors, it is first necessary to determine whether these symptoms represent a departure from normal development. In their study of childhood rituals, Leonard, Goldberger, Rapoport, Cheslow, and Swedo (1990) reviewed the literature on normal developmental rituals and childhood superstitions. These behaviors were reported to be common in children starting at a young age, and there did not appear to be an increased risk of OCD among those youngsters who evidenced normal childhood rituals and superstitions. However, there are a number of important differences between these common behaviors and symptoms of OCD. Whereas normal rituals (as presented in Table 1.1) tend to begin at a very young age and serve a positive function in social and emotional development, symptoms of OCD typically develop after the age of 7, are emotionally distressing, interfere significantly with daily functioning, and involve distinctly different behaviors (e.g., washing, checking). Although stress and anxiety can increase superstitious behavior as well as symptoms of OCD, the content of childhood superstitions differs from that of OCD. Superstitious behaviors occur across the life span and typically are believed to bring good luck or prevent bad luck. For example, finding a four-leaf clover or a penny, carrying a rabbit's foot, or wearing lucky socks while playing baseball are common superstitions thought to bring good luck. Bad luck is thought to occur if one steps on a crack, breaks a mirror, walks under a ladder, or crosses the path of a black cat. Obsessive-compulsive symptoms, as described previously, rarely involve these common superstitious themes.

Once it is clear that a child's presenting symptoms represent a significant departure from normal development, one faces the task of making an appropriate diagnostic determination. A number of psychiatric problems involve persistent worries, preoccupations, or behaviors; however, OCD is not diagnosed if the content of these symptoms is restricted to another mental disorder. Differentiating between OCD and certain disorders is relatively straightforward. If repetitive behavior involves only hair pulling, then Trichotillomania is diagnosed. A movement disorder (e.g., Tourette's Disorder, Chronic Motor Tic Disorder) is diagnosed when sudden and rapid motor or vocal acts are repeated, such as facial grimacing or throat clearing. In Anorexia and Bulimia, preoccupations are circumscribed to food, weight, and exercise issues, whereas preoccupations focus solely on physical appearance in Body Dysmorphic Disorder. If excessive concern with illness is present without accompanying rituals, a diagnosis of Hypochondriasis should be considered if the predominant feature is a fear that one has a disease, whereas a diagnosis of Specific Phobia (of illness) would be more appropriate for one who fears developing an illness.

Several other disorders are characterized by the presence of recurrent behaviors that are sometimes viewed as "compulsive." However, if the performance of these behaviors is perceived as pleasurable, then they are not defined as compulsions. For example, if an individual abuses alcohol, diagnosis with a Substance Use Disorder would be appropriate. If an adolescent cannot control impulses to bet his entire allowance on the outcome of the high school football games, a diagnosis of Pathological Gambling may be considered. Similarly, repetitive sexually arousing fantasies, urges, or behaviors that cause significant distress or impairment may warrant diagnosis of a Paraphilia. Finally, children with Disruptive Behavior Disorders may display repetitive thoughts or behaviors (e.g., preoccupation with getting their own way, persistent demanding or controlling behaviors, recurrent acts of stealing or aggression). These behaviors typically are performed to obtain a desired outcome (e.g., attention, money, control) rather than to alleviate anxiety.

Pervasive Developmental Disorders (e.g., Asperger's Disorder, Autistic Disorder) also share certain features with OCD. Children diagnosed with Pervasive Developmental Disorders display repetitive and stereotyped patterns of behavior, interests, or activities that may be mistaken for obsessions or compulsions. For example, children with Autistic Disorder frequently engage in self-stimulating behaviors (e.g., flapping hands, spinning objects), and those with Asperger's Disorder commonly exhibit preoccupations with narrowly focused interests (e.g., knowing everything there is to know about dinosaurs and restricting communication with others to that one topic). In addition to the obvious differences in content, these behaviors differ from rituals commonly associated with OCD in that they are not performed to reduce anxiety or to prevent anticipated negative consequences.

Despite similar diagnostic labels, essential features of OCD and Obsessive-Compulsive Personality Disorder (OCPD) are different. OCPD does not involve obsessive thoughts or ritualistic behaviors but, rather, a pervasive pattern of preoccupation with orderliness, perfectionism, and control. For example, individuals with a diagnosis of OCPD might be unable to complete a project at work because of overconcern with unimportant details. They may also be unwilling to delegate parts of the task to others whom they assume would be unable to meet their unrealistically high standards. Given the long-standing nature of the symptoms associated with personality disorders, it is not surprising that OCPD rarely is diagnosed in children.

It can be difficult to differentiate between worries, ruminations, and obsessions. Worries typically involve concerns about everyday or real-life problems. Such concerns are often seen in children and adolescents with Separation Anxiety Disorder (e.g., worry about being separated from parents), Social Phobia (e.g., worry about giving a speech in front of the class), Specific Phobia (e.g., worry about being stung by a bee), and Generalized Anxiety Disorder (e.g., worry about what will happen in the future). Ruminations consist of brooding thoughts, which may occur during episodes of Major Depression or Dysthymia and are congruent with the affective content of these disorders (e.g., pessimistic or morbid thoughts). As defined earlier, obsessions differ in content and function from both worries and ruminations.

Distinguishing between OCD and emerging psychotic disorders in adolescents may also present a challenge to diagnosticians. Distorted thought processes appear to occur along a continuum from obsessions, to obsessions with overvalued ideation, to delusions. Typical obsessions are disturbing to the adolescent and are viewed as illogical and disruptive to routine functioning. When individuals display overvalued ideation associated with OCD, they may have difficulty realizing that their fears are unrealistic when they are experiencing high levels of stress. However, when they are not confronting an anxiety-arousing situation, they may be able to recognize the senseless nature of their thoughts. For example, when an adolescent with overvalued ideation is being asked to touch a doorknob that she thinks is contaminated, she may truly believe that she will become ill and die, even though she can identify this belief as illogical at other times. In contrast, an adolescent with Delusional Disorder or Schizophrenia demonstrates impaired reality testing that is not dependent on heightened anxiety states. Although the content of delusions may be similar to obsessions (e.g., somatic concerns, contamination), those with a Delusional Disorder possess a firm and unwavering belief in the validity of their distorted thoughts and alter their lives accordingly. Individuals with Schizophrenia are likely to present with several additional symptoms (e.g., hallucinations, disorganized speech, blunted affect, extreme social withdrawal) that rarely are found in those with OCD.

We have evaluated a number of adolescents with psychotic disorders who previously were misdiagnosed with OCD because they displayed odd behaviors resembling compulsive rituals. Fran was a 17-year-old girl who was believed to have checking rituals because she repeatedly looked at herself in the mirror to make sure that someone had not placed razor blades in her hair. Gregg, a 16-year-old boy, initially appeared to have contamination fears. He worried about being poisoned and refused to eat anything unless his mother tasted it first. At mealtimes, he opened his mouth only slightly while eating to avoid ingesting poison and hunched over his plate to guard its contents from contamination. Tony, a 14-year-old male, kept all of his school papers in his backpack. He would not throw the papers away, refused to allow others to see them, and carried them with him at all times. This behavior had been viewed as a hoarding ritual. In each of these cases, a thorough functional analysis revealed that these behaviors were prompted by paranoid ideation. Fran and Gregg were convinced that others were trying to harm them, and Tony feared that people were attempting to obtain personal information that could later be used against him. These examples highlight the importance of conducting a complete mental status examination as part of a routine assessment of youth with OCD. Failure to do so may lead to misdiagnosis and implementation of inappropriate treatments. Although differential diagnosis may not pose a problem once psychotic symptoms are fully developed, it is likely to be a more difficult task with adolescents, whose symptoms are just beginning to emerge. Thus, careful monitoring of symptoms may need to occur over time to make an accurate diagnostic determination.

COMORBIDITY

The majority of children and adolescents with OCD present with a lifetime history of another psychiatric disorder. The most common comorbid diagnoses involve anxiety and mood disorders. Rates of comorbid anxiety disorders range from 15% to 75%, and mood disorders have been found to coexist in 25% to 38% of youth with OCD (Flament et al., 1990; Flament et al., 1988; Hanna, 1995; Last et al., 1992; Toro, Cervera, Osejo, & Salamero, 1992). Comorbid disruptive behavior disorders are evidenced in 6% to 18% of children and adolescents with OCD (Flament et al., 1990; Last et al., 1992; Toro et al., 1992; Zohar et al., 1992). Finally, only 15% of adolescents with OCD in a community sample were diagnosed with comorbid Obsessive-Compulsive Personality Disorder (OCPD; Flament et al., 1988).

Although it has been suggested that there is a close link between OCD and Tourette's syndrome (TS; a neuropsychiatric disorder characterized by a combination of motor and vocal tics) (e.g., Rapoport, 1991), the extent of this relationship appears to differ depending on the sample being assessed. Whereas OCD has been reported in up to 42% of youth diagnosed with TS (Apter et al., 1993; Grad, Pelcovitz, Olson, Matthews, & Grad, 1987), TS has been found in only 0% to 15% of those with OCD diagnoses (Flament et al., 1988; Hanna, 1995; Toro et al., 1992; Zohar et al., 1992). Other movement disorders (i.e., Transient Tic Disorder, Chronic Motor or Vocal Tic Disorder) have been found in 13% to 20% of youth with OCD (Hanna, 1995; Zohar et al., 1992).

Overlap between OCD and Trichotillomania has been suggested by similar positive treatment results with antiobsessional medications and by family history data that show increased rates of OCD among first-degree relatives of those with Trichotillomania (Swedo, Leonard, Rapoport, et al., 1989). However, in the only study to examine comorbidity in children with Trichotillomania, Reeve, Bernstein, and Christenson (1992) found no cases of OCD in 10 children and adolescents with Trichotillomania. Given that youth with OCD are likely to have comorbid psychiatric disorders, it is essential that one complete a thorough diagnostic assessment to identify these conditions. Moreover, it may be necessary to provide adjunctive therapies to address concurrent symptoms as part of a comprehensive treatment package for youth with OCD. For example, the immediate use of an antidepressant medication may be necessary to effectively treat a youngster who presents with severe depressive symptoms in addition to OCD.

SUMMARY

In this chapter, information regarding the diagnosis of OCD was presented. Detailed descriptions of the most common types of obsessions and compulsions were provided with examples of how they might present in children and adolescents. On the basis of a brief overview of biological and psychological models of the etiology of OCD, it was concluded that certain individuals are likely to have a biological predisposition to develop OCD, although there is no conclusive evidence regarding factors that may trigger the onset of symptoms in those at risk. Negative reinforcement was implicated as the factor responsible for the maintenance of OCD symptoms. The epidemiological literature was reviewed; however, due to the paucity of research available with this population, no definitive conclusions could be drawn regarding prevalence, onset of symptoms, or prognosis of childhood OCD. Guidelines for differential diagnosis were provided, and the importance of assessing and treating common comorbid conditions was highlighted.

2

ASSESSMENT

The assessment of childhood OCD is a challenging process that requires gathering information from multiple sources across different settings using a variety of methods. This chapter will describe an assortment of techniques for assessing OCD. These include diagnostic interviews, clinician-rated instruments, self-report questionnaires, self-monitoring, and behavioral observation. In addition, practical guidelines for selecting appropriate assessment strategies will be provided.

DIAGNOSTIC INTERVIEWS

Structured and Semistructured Diagnostic Interviews

Although there is no standardized diagnostic interview designed specifically to assess OCD in children and adolescents, many of the available structured and semistructured interviews include questions relevant to the diagnosis. These interviews typically have parallel versions that are administered to children and parents separately. Each version consists of initial screening questions regarding the major diagnostic categories. If the respondent positively endorses the screening items for OCD, the interviewer proceeds with further questions about specific obsessive-compulsive symptoms.

The major difference between structured and semistructured instruments is the extent to which clinical judgment is required and flexibility is allowed during the interview process. Structured diagnostic interviews such as the Diagnostic Interview for Children and Adolescents-Revised (DICA-R; Welner, Reich, Herjanic, & Campbell, 1987) and the Diagnostic Interview Schedule for Children-Revised (DISC-R; Schwab-Stone et al., 1993) typically limit the interviewer to a series of specific yes-no questions. For example, in the parent version of the DICA-R, the

TABLE 2.1 Scoring Criteria for Severity of Compulsions Using the K-SADS

Rating	Label	Criteria
1	Not at all	No symptoms present.
2	Slight	Occasional ritualistic acts but unclear if clinically significant. "Games" that child can start and stop at will.
3	Mild to Moderate	Definite compulsions; cause some effect on functioning or distress or are time-consuming, taking more than 1 hour per day.
4	Severe	Frequent compulsions with considerable impairment in social or role functioning or daily routine, or marked distress, or are *very* time-consuming.

initial screening question used to assess for the presence of compulsions is "Does he often find himself doing things that seem unnecessary such as touching things over and over or washing over and over?" In contrast, semistructured interviews, such as the Schedule for Affective Disorders and Schizophrenia for School-Age Children (K-SADS; Puig-Antich & Chambers, 1982) and the Anxiety Disorders Interview Schedule for Children (K-ADIS; Silverman & Nelles, 1988), allow much more flexibility for the interviewer. As an example, the K-SADS requires the interviewer to rate the severity of a variety of compulsions on a 4-point scale (see Table 2.1). Suggestions are provided regarding how to phrase questions in order to obtain the information necessary to rate the symptoms. However, interviewers are given the freedom to select as many or as few questions as deemed necessary to make their clinical judgments. Both closed- and open-ended questions may be asked of the respondent. For example, the following sequence of questions might be used to assess compulsions: "Do you have to arrange things in your room in a particular way?" . . . "Why do you do this?" . . . "Do you try to stop yourself from doing it?" . . . "What happens then?"

Structured and semistructured interviews provide a thorough review of all major diagnostic categories, thus allowing one to determine the diagnosis of OCD as well as any comorbid diagnoses. The structured nature of these instruments increases the ability of independent raters to arrive at the same diagnostic conclusions for a given child, thus improving interrater reliability. Although semistructured interviews must be conducted by professional diagnosticians, structured interviews can be administered using computers or trained paraprofessionals. The major disadvantage of structured and semistructured interviews is that they require an enormous amount of time to complete. For instance, it may take in excess of 3 hours to administer both child and parent versions of the K-SADS.

Unstructured Clinical Interviews

In clinical practice, an unstructured interview is the most common method used to gather data regarding the history of presenting problems. If conducted by clinicians who are knowledgeable about childhood psychopathology, these interviews can elicit the information necessary to make diagnostic determinations regarding the presence of OCD and any comorbid conditions. Typically, they can be performed more quickly than structured or semistructured interviews; however, they are not likely to be appropriate for research purposes due to their nonstandardized administration and reliance on subjective clinical judgment.

CLINICIAN-RATED INSTRUMENTS

Global Symptom Rating Scales

A number of instruments have been developed to elicit clinicians' judgments regarding the global severity of OCD symptoms in adults. For example, the NIMH Global Obsessive Compulsive Scale (NIMH-OC; Insel et al., 1983) requires the clinician to describe the current clinical state of the patient using a 15-point scale (see Table 2.2). The O-C Rating Scale (Rapoport, Elkins, & Mikkelsen, 1980) and the Obsessive-Compulsive subscale of the Comprehensive Psychopathological Rating Scale (CPRS-OC; Asberg, Montgomery, Perris, Schalling, & Sedvall, 1978) are similar clinician-rated measures. Although these instruments were all developed for adults, they have been used routinely in treatment outcome studies conducted with children and adolescents. The primary advantages of this type of scale are that they can be completed rapidly and that they provide guidelines for making quantifiable ratings of global symptom severity. These ratings can then be used to compare the severity of OCD symptoms across different individuals or within a single person over time. Unfortunately, no information is currently available on the psychometric properties of these instruments when used with children and adolescents. Global symptom ratings are not designed to provide information regarding specific

TABLE 2.2 Scoring Criteria Adapted From the NIMH Global Obsessive-Compulsive Scale

Score	Label	Criteria
1-3	Within Normal Range	Mild symptoms. Person spends little time resisting them. Almost no interference in daily activity.
4-6	Subclinical Obsessive Compulsive Behavior	Mild symptoms that are noticeable to patient and observer, cause mild interference in patient's life and may be resisted for a minimal period of time. Easily tolerated by others.
7-9	Clinical Obsessive Compulsive Behavior	Symptoms that cause significant interference in patient's life and that require a great deal of conscious energy to resist. Requires some help from others to function in daily activity.
10-12	Severe Obsessive Compulsive Behavior	Symptoms that are crippling to the patient and that interfere to the extent that daily activity is "an active struggle." Patient may spend full-time resisting symptoms. Requires much help from others to function.
13-15	Very Severe Obsessive Compulsive Behavior	Symptoms that completely cripple patient to the extent that close supervision is required for all activities of daily living. Requires help from others to complete even basic tasks.

obsessive-compulsive symptomatology, nor do they elicit information sufficient to determine whether a diagnosis of OCD is warranted.

Children's Yale-Brown Obsessive Compulsive Scale (CY-BOCS)

The Children's Yale-Brown Obsessive Compulsive Scale (CY-BOCS; Goodman et al., 1986; Hardin et al., 1991) is a clinician-rated instrument for assessing the severity of OCD symptoms (see Appendix A). The CY-BOCS is the child and adolescent version of the widely used Yale-Brown Obsessive Compulsive Scale (Y-BOCS; Goodman et al., 1989). A symptom checklist is used to identify the child's presenting complaints. The symptom checklist includes obsessions (aggressive, contamination, magical thoughts, hoarding/saving, religious, somatic, and miscellaneous) and compulsions (cleaning/washing, checking, repeating, counting, ordering/arranging, hoarding/collecting, rituals involving other people, and miscellaneous). Following administration of the symptom checklist, 10 items are rated on 5-point scales to assess symptom severity. Items include time occupied by obsessive thoughts, interference due to obses-

TABLE 2.3 Sample Scoring Criteria for the CY-BOCS

Time Occupied by Obsessive Thoughts:

How much time is occupied by obsessive thoughts?
How much time do you spend thinking about these things?
How frequently do these thoughts occur?

Rating	Label	Criteria
0	None	
1	Mild	Less than 1 hour/day or occasional intrusion
2	Moderate	1-3 hours/day or frequent intrusion
3	Severe	3-8 hours/day or very frequent intrusion
4	Extreme	Greater than 8 hours/day or near constant intrusion

Degree of Control Over Compulsive Behavior:

How strong is the drive to perform the compulsive behavior?
How much control do you have over the compulsions?
How strong is the feeling that you have to carry out the habit(s)?
When you try to fight them what happens?
How much control do you have over the habits?

Rating	Label	Criteria
0	Complete control	
1	Much control	Experiences pressure to perform the behavior but usually able to exercise voluntary control over it
2	Moderate control	Strong pressure to perform behavior, can control it only with difficulty
3	Little control	Very strong drive to perform behavior, must be carried to completion, can only delay with difficulty
4	No control	Drive to perform behavior experienced as completely involuntary and overpowering, rarely able to even momentarily delay activity

sive thoughts, distress associated with obsessive thoughts, resistance against obsessions, degree of control over obsessive thoughts, time spent performing compulsive behaviors, interference due to compulsive behaviors, distress associated with compulsive behavior, resistance against compulsions, and degree of control over compulsive behavior. Examples of the rating criteria can be found in Table 2.3.

The CY-BOCS enables the clinician to complete a thorough review of obsessive-compulsive symptoms in a manner that is appropriate to the developmental level of children and adolescents. In addition to providing a measure of the overall severity of symptoms, it elicits more specific information regarding the independent effects of obsessions and compulsions on the child's functioning. Symptom severity can be assessed over time with repeated administrations of the CY-BOCS, allowing one to monitor the effects of treatment. A diagnosis of OCD can be determined rather quickly based on the information obtained from the CY-BOCS. Although no published data currently exist regarding the reliability and validity of the CY-BOCS, the Y-BOCS has been described as the instrument of choice for rating OCD symptoms in adults (March, Leonard, & Swedo, 1995).

SELF-REPORT QUESTIONNAIRES

Maudsley Obsessional-Compulsive Inventory (MOCI)

The Maudsley Obsessional-Compulsive Inventory (MOCI; Hodgson & Rachman, 1977) consists of 30 true-false questions designed to assess OCD symptoms in adults. Sample items include the following: "I take rather a long time to complete my washing in the morning," "I do not use a great deal of antiseptics," "Hanging and folding my clothes at night does not take up a lot of my time," and "I have a very strict conscience." The MOCI yields a total obsessive-compulsive score and four subscale scores (checking, cleaning, slowness, doubting). High scores on the MOCI have been found to be related to specific obsessive-compulsive symptoms elicited through interview assessment of a non-clinical sample of young adults (Sternberger & Burns, 1990). Only one study has evaluated the MOCI in an adolescent sample. Clark and Bolton (1985a) administered the MOCI to a small group of adolescents with OCD and to a matched group of adolescents with other anxiety problems and found that those with OCD obtained significantly higher total obsessive-compulsive scores than the anxious controls. No differences were obtained between the two groups on any of the four subscales of the MOCI.

Clearly, there are a number of problems associated with using an adult self-report instrument such as the MOCI with children and adolescents. The wording and content of questions are not developmentally appropriate. For example, children are not likely to be familiar with terms such as *strict conscience* and *antiseptic*. In addition, typical childhood activities that may be affected by OCD symptoms are not assessed (e.g., schoolwork, playing with toys, interacting with parents). Furthermore, no normative or psychometric data are available on the MOCI for child and adolescent samples. Thus, it is not recommended that the MOCI be used to assess OCD symptoms in youth.

Leyton Obsessional Inventory—Child Version (LOI-CV)

The Leyton Obsessional Inventory-Child Version (LOI-CV; Berg, Rapoport, & Flament, 1986) is a modified version of the Leyton Obsessional Inventory (LOI; Cooper, 1970), a scale devised to assess OCD symptoms in adults. The LOI-CV consists of 44 questions that assess the presence of obsessive thoughts and compulsive behaviors (see Appendix B). Sample items include the following: "Do thoughts or words ever keep going over and over in your mind?" "Do you ever have to check doors, cupboards or windows to make sure that they are really shut?" "Do you ever clean your room or your toys when they are not really dirty in order to make them extra clean?" "Do you have to dress or undress in a certain order?" "Do you ever have to do things over and over a certain number of times before they seem quite right?" "Is your room crowded with old toys, string, boxes, games, and clothes just because you think they might be needed some day?" The LOI-CV is administered using a card sort procedure that enables one to obtain information about the total number of OCD symptoms (yes score), the child's attempts to resist symptoms (resistance score), and the extent of functional impairment (interference score). Each question is written on an index card, and the child is first asked to sort the cards into two piles based on his or her answers. The total number of symptoms endorsed makes up the yes score. The child must then indicate the degree of resistance and interference present for each of the symptoms that was endorsed. Symptom cards are sorted into the following resistance categories, which are scored using a 5-point scale: 0 = My thoughts and habits are quite sensible and reasonable; 1 = This is just a habit, and I just do it without really thinking about it; 2 = I often realize I don't have to do this but don't bother to try to stop; 3 = I know that this is not necessary, that I don't have to do this, and I try to stop; and 4 = What I do bothers me a lot, and I try very hard to stop. Scores for each symptom card are summed to obtain the resistance score. Finally, symptom cards are sorted into the following interference categories and are scored using a 4-point scale: 0 = My habit does not stop me from other things I want to do; 1 = This stops me a little or wastes some of my time; 2 = This stops me from doing other things and wastes a lot of my time; and 3 = This habit stops me from doing a lot of things and wastes a lot of my time. Scores for each symptom card are summed to obtain the interference score.

Berg, Rapoport, and Flament (1986) reported that resistance and interference scores on the LOI-CV distinguished adolescents with OCD from both psychiatric and normal controls. Although adolescents with OCD obtained higher yes scores than normal controls, their scores did not differ from those of psychiatric controls. The authors reported excellent test-retest reliability over a 4-week period for yes ($r = .96$), resistance ($r = .97$), and interference scores ($r = .94$). Furthermore, these scores were found to be sensitive to drug treatment effects, lending support for the validity of the LOI-CV.

A brief self-report version of the LOI-CV was developed as a survey form for epidemiological research (Berg, Whitaker, Davies, Flament, & Rapoport, 1988). The survey form includes 20 items drawn from the original LOI-CV. As with the original LOI-CV, the survey form yields a yes score and an interference score. Berg et al. (1988) administered the survey form to a sample of over 5,000 high school students. Good internal consistency was reported for this version of the LOI-CV (Cronbach's $\alpha = 0.81$). No age differences were noted, but females obtained significantly higher scores than males. The average yes score was 7.7 for females and 6.0 for males. Similarly, the average interference score was 6.9 for females and 5.3 for males.

Flament et al. (1988) assessed the utility of the survey form of the LOI-CV as a method of identifying high school students with and without a diagnosis of OCD. They reported that 88% of adolescents with OCD, as determined by diagnostic interview, were able to be correctly identified as such if they obtained a yes score of greater than or equal to 15 and an interference score of greater than or equal to 25. Using these cutoff scores 77% of students without OCD were correctly classified as such. Thus, screening for OCD using the survey form resulted in 12% false negatives (adolescents who met diagnostic criteria for OCD but did not obtain high scores on the questionnaire) and 23% false positives (adolescents who did not meet diagnostic criteria for OCD but did obtain high scores on the questionnaire). These results suggest that the survey form of the LOI-CV may be helpful as an initial screening device for identifying OCD in adolescents.

In sum, the card sort and survey form versions of the LOI-CV provide psychometrically sound data regarding the presence and severity of specific obsessive-compulsive symptoms. These instruments are designed specifically for use with children and adolescents, and they can be completed quickly and easily. Thus, if administered repeatedly over time, the LOI-CV can be used to monitor the course of symptoms or the effects of treatment. Scores obtained on the LOI-CV, however, have not been found to correlate significantly with global clinician ratings of OCD symptom severity (Berg et al., 1988). One must keep in mind that the LOI-CV is not designed to determine the presence or absence of a diagnosis of OCD. Nonetheless, the survey form may be a useful screening tool for identifying those youth who require further diagnostic evaluation.

SELF-MONITORING

Self-monitoring can be an excellent method to gather more detailed information about the frequency and severity of OCD symptoms. Shapiro (1984) defined self-monitoring as any procedure in which a child records the presence of behavior. This can be accomplished in several different ways. For example, children can be asked to write narrative descriptions of their behavior, to complete paper-and-pencil data sheets specifically designed to record target behaviors, or to use mechanical counting devices to keep track of the frequency of these behaviors. It is essential that one provide a clear explanation of what the child is to monitor and how such monitoring is to be done. Target behaviors should be objectively defined, using terms that the child can understand.

It also can be helpful to have children self-monitor the level of discomfort that is associated with their symptoms. Level of distress can be rated quickly and easily using individually determined Subjective Units of Discomfort Scales (SUDS; Wolpe, 1990). The complexity of the SUDS scale should take into account the child's age and level of cognitive maturity. For example, a 6-year-old may be able to use a 3-point scale, anchored with pictures, to indicate "no," "some," or "a lot" of anxiety, whereas an adolescent may be able to understand a SUDS scale that ranges from 0 (completely relaxed) to 100 (completely panic-stricken). Examples of self-monitoring forms tailored for young children and adolescents are illustrated in Tables 2.4 and 2.5, respectively. In both cases, the forms are designed to self-monitor contamination obsessions and handwashing compulsions.

Children are most likely to comply with requests to self-monitor when they are given a rationale for doing so and are involved actively in determining how, what, and when to self-monitor. Although it may

TABLE 2.4 Sample Self-Monitoring Form for a 6-Year-Old Child With Handwashing Rituals

Please fill out this form every time you go into the bathroom.

I went into the bathroom because I touched something germy.	I washed my hands . . .	I worried about germs . . .		
☐ Yes ☐ No	☐ Once ☐ More than once	☺ Not at all	Some	☹ A lot
☐ Yes ☐ No	☐ Once ☐ More than once	☺ Not at all	Some	☹ A lot
☐ Yes ☐ No	☐ Once ☐ More than once	☺ Not at all	Some	☹ A lot
☐ Yes ☐ No	☐ Once ☐ More than once	☺ Not at all	Some	☹ A lot
☐ Yes ☐ No	☐ Once ☐ More than once	☺ Not at all	Some	☹ A lot

be tempting to design a comprehensive self-monitoring system that includes all information that could possibly be useful for treatment, it will be very difficult to get a child to comply with such a complex and overwhelming task. The clinician should select a small number of target behaviors for self-monitoring that are most relevant for evaluation and treatment. To increase motivation and compliance with self-monitoring tasks, it is helpful to provide special rewards to the child contingent on completion of these tasks.

Self-monitoring data provide information that can be used to identify specific and individualized targets for intervention and to evaluate treatment efficacy over time. If these data are summarized and presented in graph form, a picture of treatment progress is created that may serve to motivate youngsters to achieve therapy goals. The major drawback to the use of self-monitoring is that it is time-consuming and requires a great deal of compliance from the child. At times, obsessive-compulsive symptoms may interfere with the child's ability to complete self-monitoring forms. For example, children with obsessions involving the need for symmetry and exactness in their handwriting may engage in time-consuming perfectionistic rituals (e.g., erasing and rewriting data repeat-

TABLE 2.5 Sample Self-Monitoring Form for an Adolescent With Handwashing Rituals

Please fill out this form every time you wash your hands.

Date and time	What were you doing immediately before you washed your hands?	What were you thinking about?	Before washing your hands, how anxious were you about getting AIDS? (0 = completely relaxed, 100 = completely panic-stricken)	How many minutes did you spend washing your hands?	After washing your hands, how anxious were you about getting AIDS? (0 → 100)

edly) that would preclude the use of self-monitoring. However, it is recommended that self-monitoring be included as part of a comprehensive assessment of obsessive-compulsive symptomatology whenever possible.

BEHAVIORAL OBSERVATION

By their very nature, a number of symptoms experienced by children with OCD can be observed by the clinician during the course of an initial evaluation. For example, it is not uncommon for a child with contamination obsessions to demonstrate avoidance behaviors by refusing to shake hands with the clinician when introduced or by refraining from touching the office doorknob. Similarly, an adolescent with hoarding rituals may collect pamphlets from the waiting room or pick up stray paper clips and staples from the floor. Rituals also may be observed during the completion of assessment tasks, such as self-monitoring forms (e.g., the child with perfectionistic behaviors as described above) or the card sort version of the LOI-CV (e.g., the child who is unable to complete resistance and interference ratings due to avoidance of choosing the "unlucky number two").

It can be very helpful to observe children with OCD in natural settings to see how symptoms are manifested outside of the confines of the clinician's office. Often, children are unable to describe clearly all of the rituals they perform over the course of a day. Direct observation of the child at home or school can allow for a more thorough understanding of the context and content of symptoms. For example, one may discover that a child is more symptomatic when interacting with one parent than the other, is able to refrain from rituals at school more than at home, or is displaying rituals that were not acknowledged during the clinical interview. This underscores the need for assessments to be conducted across settings.

Aside from providing descriptive information, behavioral observations can be conducted to obtain objective data regarding the frequency of overt symptomatology. Although no observational rating scales currently exist specifically for this purpose, such instruments can be designed to provide data needed for a particular child. The complexity of behavioral observation rating scales can vary from a simple frequency count of target behaviors to a complicated sequential analysis of the child's behavior over time. Barton and Ascione (1984) highlight several factors that must be considered when developing a behavioral observation rating scale, including the need for operationally defined rating criteria, sufficient observer training, and adequate interrater reliability. Behavioral observations can be particularly useful when children are secretive about reporting their symptoms or when they are unable to accurately self-monitor due to their developmental level or symptom interference. Parents or other adults can be trained to conduct behavioral observations, thus allowing information about the child's symptoms to be gathered in a variety of settings and at times when the clinician is not present. A limitation to this method is that only overt behaviors can be observed and rated. Thus, information about cognitive events, such as obsessions or mental rituals, cannot be obtained. Furthermore, some children inhibit their rituals in the presence of observers, making behavioral observations impossible. Although the use of behavioral observation to obtain descriptive information is relatively easy, it can be cumbersome to develop and implement observational rating systems designed to gather reliable quantitative data needed for research purposes.

PRACTICAL ASSESSMENT GUIDELINES: PUTTING THE PIECES TOGETHER

It is obvious from the descriptions of the various assessment techniques provided in this chapter that each method has pros and cons associated with its use. The challenge for the clinician is to select those instruments that will best answer the assessment questions that are posed. These questions may vary depending on the purpose of the evaluation. There are three primary purposes of assessment: (a) to make diagnostic determinations, (b) to complete a functional analysis of presenting symptoms, and (c) to monitor the clinical course and treatment efficacy or both over time.

Diagnosis

The manner in which diagnostic determinations are made varies depending on the nature of the referral base and the setting in which one practices. Given that OCD occurs in less than 2% of youth who present for treatment in general inpatient and outpatient facilities (Hollingsworth et al., 1980; Judd, 1965), it may not be practical or useful for clinicians in these settings to routinely conduct a thorough diagnostic evaluation of obsessive-compulsive symptomatology. However, all youth who present for psychiatric evaluation should be screened for the presence of OCD regardless of the referral question. This can be accomplished by incorporating a few screening questions, such as those included in structured diagnostic interviews, as part of the initial intake interview. For example, even though a child may present for an evaluation for Attention-Deficit Hyperactivity Disorder (ADHD), he or she should be asked about obsessions and compulsions. To screen for the presence of obsessive thoughts, one might ask the following series of questions: "Do you ever have thoughts that keep popping into your head? Thoughts that are hard to get rid of, even though you might want to? Like thinking a lot about germs or worrying that something really bad is going to happen?" The presence of compulsions can be assessed briefly by asking the following questions: "Are there certain things that you do over and over again or in some special way? Like washing your hands many times, more than other kids do? Or checking things over and over, like going back to make sure things are unplugged or turned off, more than just once or twice? Or do you have any habits or routines that you have to do in a certain way?" If the child responds positively to these screening questions, then a comprehensive evaluation of OCD is warranted.

Behavior rating scales that generally are given as part of routine clinical evaluations may also be used to screen for OCD because they often contain some items assessing the presence of obsessive thoughts and ritualistic behaviors. If these items are endorsed, further evaluation of specific obsessive-compulsive symptoms is indicated. For example, the Child Behavior Checklist (Achenbach, 1991) asks parents to rate the presence of the following behaviors: can't get his or her mind off certain thoughts (obsessions), repeats certain acts over and over (compulsions), stores up things he or she doesn't need, too concerned with neatness or cleanliness, feels he or she needs to be perfect, and fears he or she might think or do something bad.

In addition to the procedures described above, it is recommended that the 20-item LOI-CV be administered routinely to children who present for evaluation of anxiety symptoms. Because nearly 15% of youth with anxiety disorders are diagnosed with OCD (Last et al., 1992) and rates of comorbid anxiety disorders are high among youngsters with OCD (Flament et al., 1990; Flament et al., 1988; Hanna, 1995; Last et al., 1992; Toro et al., 1992), it is worthwhile to complete a more thorough assessment of obsessions and compulsions than is possible with global behavior checklists. If high scores are obtained on the LOI-CV, further investigation is warranted to determine whether criteria for the diagnosis of OCD are met.

When youngsters are referred specifically for evaluation of obsessive-compulsive behaviors or when it has been established that such behaviors are present via the screening procedures described above, the clinician must gather detailed information regarding the content, frequency, and severity of symptoms to confirm the diagnosis of OCD. The card sort version of the LOI-CV can be used to obtain comprehensive self-report data about the child's symptom profile. Completion of the CY-BOCS is recommended as the final step in the process of verifying the diagnosis of OCD.

Although not necessary in clinical practice, completion of a structured or semistructured diagnostic interview is the method of choice when establishing diagnoses for research purposes. Although these instruments confirm the presence or absence of the diagnosis of OCD, they do not provide quantitative information about symptomatology. Therefore, it is recommended that the CY-BOCS and LOI-CV also be included as part of the assessment protocol in research studies of OCD.

Functional Analysis

Another purpose of assessment is to conduct a functional analysis of the child's OCD symptoms. A functional analysis involves determining the role of antecedent and consequent variables in the manifestation of symptomatology. The assessment must include an evaluation of the child's functioning in a variety of situations, including at home, in school, with family members, and with peers. The primary goal of the functional analysis is to determine whether there are any patterns associated with variations in symptomatology. Events that serve to trigger or maintain the obsessive-compulsive behaviors can often be identified. The clinician needs to obtain information about the circumstances under which symptoms are likely to occur or become worse, as well as those in which the child experiences relief from symptoms. It is also important to gain an understanding of what happens when the child engages in obsessive-compulsive behaviors. The responses of parents, teachers, and peers should be considered, because these individuals may inadvertently reinforce the display of symptoms. Children may get secondary gains from the attention they get from others when they perform rituals or express their obsessive thoughts (e.g., a child who receives much reassurance from a concerned parent); or they might be permitted to avoid their responsibilities (e.g., an adolescent whose parents don't require her to do her homework or chores because she is "too sick"). A number of other factors are likely to influence the expression of OCD symptoms and should be taken into consideration when completing a functional analysis and developing a treatment plan. Examples of these variables include the presence of comorbid psychiatric conditions, the strengths and weaknesses of the family system (e.g., degree of social support, level of motivation, willingness to comply with treatment recommendations, presence of parental psychopathology), socioeconomic factors (e.g., parental employment status and educational level), and cultural issues (e.g., expectations about family roles and boundaries). The assessment methods most suitable for gathering the information required for a functional analysis are unstructured clinical interviews, self-monitoring, and behavioral observations.

Symptom Monitoring

A third purpose of assessment is to monitor the course of symptoms over time. Typically, this is done to evaluate the effectiveness of treatment interventions. Ideally, a variety of assessment methods should be used to monitor symptoms throughout the course of treatment (see Table 2.6). Information should be obtained from multiple sources who are familiar with the child's functioning across different settings. Given that the CY-BOCS is the most comprehensive clinician-rated assessment device, it is the method of choice to monitor changes in symptomatology. Due to time constraints, however, clinicians may opt to use global symptom rating scales to obtain frequent (e.g., weekly) measures of symptom severity during treatment. Nonetheless, the CY-BOCS should be administered at pretreatment, posttreatment, and follow-up if it is impractical to do so on a more frequent basis. Similarly, the card sort version of the LOI-CV provides a comprehensive picture of self-reported symptom severity that can be administered on the same schedule as the CY-BOCS. Ongoing assessment of treatment progress from the child's perspective can be ascertained from self-monitoring data. Behavioral observations can also be conducted on an ongoing basis to provide information regarding the course of OCD symptoms.

SUMMARY

In this chapter, a variety of strategies for assessing childhood OCD were presented. The importance of including a thorough diagnostic interview was emphasized, although the type of interview will vary

TABLE 2.6 Suggested Assessment Schedule for Monitoring Treatment Progress

Assessment Device	Time			
	Pretreatment	During Treatment	Post-treatment	Follow-Up
Diagnostic interview	X			
CY-BOCS	X		X	X
Global Symptom Rating Scale	X	X (weekly)	X	X
LOI-CV	X		X	X
Self-Monitoring	X	X (daily)	X	X
Behavioral observation	X	X (varies)	X	X

depending on the needs of the clinician. Global symptom rating scales and the CY-BOCS were described as useful clinician-rated instruments for assessing the severity of obsessive-compulsive symptoms, and the LOI-CV was presented as the most appropriate self-report measure for use with youth. Suggestions were provided regarding how to incorporate developmentally appropriate self-monitoring and behavioral observation systems to obtain more detailed information about the frequency and severity of symptoms across different settings. The chapter concluded with practical guidelines for selecting the most appropriate instruments to address the goals of the assessment (i.e., diagnosis, functional analysis, symptom monitoring).

3

TREATMENT

Psychotherapeutic, psychopharmacologic, and psychosurgical procedures all have been used to treat individuals with OCD. This chapter will review the literature regarding the application of these interventions to children and adolescents. The use of behavior therapy techniques is emphasized, and special issues related to the treatment of youth will be highlighted.

PSYCHOTHERAPEUTIC TREATMENT

Empirical Findings

The combination of exposure and response prevention (E/RP) is considered to be the treatment of choice for adults with OCD (Steketee & Cleere, 1990). Studies indicate that approximately 75% of adults treated with this combination show substantial improvement, whereas the success rates are considerably lower (20-40%) in those treated with either of these components alone. In addition, the efficacy of other treatments (e.g., cognitive therapy, relaxation training) has not compared favorably with that of E/RP (for reviews see Beck & Bourg, 1993; Stanley, 1992; Steketee, 1993).

Although psychotherapeutic treatments have been studied extensively in adults with OCD, there is limited information regarding the efficacy of such treatments in children and adolescents (for reviews see Adams, 1985; March, 1995; Wolff & Rapoport, 1988). As in the adult literature, E/RP has been the primary focus of treatment outcome studies of youth with OCD. Unfortunately, our review of the available literature on childhood OCD revealed several methodological problems that make it impossible to draw definitive conclusions about the effectiveness of psychotherapeutic treatments. Common problems included small sample sizes, lack of experimental controls, poorly defined outcome measures, and the inability to disentangle the effects of multiple treatment components. The majority of published reports were merely clinical case descriptions that did not include any measures of treatment outcome (Apter, Bernhout, & Tyano, 1984; Bolton & Turner, 1984; Dalton, 1983; Fine, 1973; Harbin, 1979; Kellerman, 1981; O'Connor, 1983; Ong & Leng, 1979; Stanley, 1980; Willmuth, 1988). In addition, there were several case studies that included measures of obsessive-compulsive symptoms at baseline and in response to treatment (Bolton, Collins, & Steinberg, 1983; Desmarais & Lavallee, 1988; Friedmann & Silvers, 1977; Green, 1980; Hallam, 1974; Harris & Wiebe, 1992; Horne, McTiernan, & Strauss, 1981; Lindley, Marks, Philpott, & Snowden, 1977; Mills, Agras, Barlow, & Mills, 1973; Morelli, 1983; Ownby, 1983). The quality of these measures, however, varied from subjective child or parent estimates of symptomatology to objective symptom counts performed by trained observers.

Only four studies have been published that used experimental designs. Three of these were single case experimental designs, whereas the fourth was a repeated measures design using a larger sample. Kearney and Silverman (1990) used an alternating treatments design, in which they attempted to compare response prevention to cognitive therapy. In this study, a 14-year-old male was treated on an outpatient basis for an obsessive fear of contracting rabies from bats and dying. He also engaged in rituals involving checking himself for drops of bat saliva and checking windows for the presence of bats. Response prevention entailed instructing the adolescent to reduce the frequency of checking rituals. Cognitive therapy involved helping him to challenge the unrealistic nature of his catastrophic thoughts by providing education about rabies and identifying evidence to refute his irrational thinking. Each treatment phase lasted 1 week, during which time two sessions were held. Treatments (A = response prevention, B = cognitive therapy) were alternated according to the following sequence: A-B-B-A-B-A-A-B-A-B-B-A. Given the nature of these treatments, however, it seems unlikely that they could be delivered independently and sequentially in this alternating design. For example, once the boy was educated about the transmission of rabies during cognitive therapy, this information would likely continue to influence his thinking and behavior during the response prevention treatment phase the next week. Given the high probability of multiple treatment interference in this study, it is impossible to compare the effects of response prevention and cognitive therapy. Nevertheless, one can evaluate the efficacy of the combination of these treatments by examining changes in target symptoms over the course of the entire study. In fact, results revealed a rapid elimination of checking rituals and decreased subjective ratings of anxiety and depression over the course of the study period; and these gains were maintained at a 6-month follow-up. This suggests that the combination of response prevention and cognitive therapy may be an effective treatment for childhood OCD.

Francis (1988) used a withdrawal design (A-B-A-B) to assess the efficacy of an extinction procedure designed to eliminate reassurance-seeking behavior in an 11-year-old boy with OCD. The youngster had obsessive thoughts about illness and death, which prompted him to ask his parents for excessive reassurance about his health (e.g., repeatedly asking if he had a tumor, questioning whether he might go blind). Parents were instructed to ignore all reassurance-seeking behavior by looking away or redirecting the conversation. Symptoms were eliminated within 6 days of treatment. When treatment was withdrawn (i.e., parents again began to attend to their son's symptoms), reassurance-seeking immediately increased to rates greater than those recorded during the initial baseline phase. With the reinstatement of treatment, it took 12 days for symptoms to be eliminated again, and the child was found to be symptom free at follow-up 1 month after completion of treatment. Results of this study provide evidence for the efficacy of extinction procedures in the elimination of compulsive reassurance-seeking, although it is unclear whether this treatment approach would result in lasting benefit, because no long-term follow-up data were provided.

March and Mulle (1995) employed a within-subject multiple baseline design to evaluate a manualized cognitive-behavioral treatment package consisting primarily of anxiety management training (AMT) and graded exposure plus response prevention (E/RP). The research participant in this study was an 8-year-old girl with contamination fears, washing and wiping rituals, reassurance-seeking, and avoidance behaviors. After 2 weeks of psychoeducation and construction of an anxiety hierarchy, AMT and E/RP were phased in at Weeks 3 and 4, respectively. E/RP was administered sequentially to the items in the anxiety hierarchy, with each item representing a separate baseline. Subjective anxiety ratings and clinician symptom ratings were noted to decrease beginning in Week 4 when E/RP was started using the first item in the hierarchy. As E/RP was applied to consecutive items on the hierarchy, improved SUDS ratings were observed. All symptoms were eliminated by the 11th week of treatment, and gains were maintained at a 6-month follow-up. The strengths of this study include its use of a well-controlled, single-case experimental design and of a treatment approach that is specified in a manualized format. Manualization of the intervention permits replication studies to be conducted in a systematic fashion. Such replication is necessary to further evaluate the utility of this promising treatment approach.

The only study to use an experimental design with more than one child was conducted by March, Mulle, and Herbel (1994). Fifteen outpatients between the ages of 8 and 18 were treated with the manualized cognitive-behavioral treatment package described above; however, all but one youngster also received concurrent treatments, including medication (14 cases), family therapy (2 cases), and supportive individual therapy (2 cases). The most common obsessions reported by these children were contamination fears, fears of harm, and symmetry urges. Washing and checking were the most common compulsions, and the majority of children evidenced significant avoidance behaviors. Clinician ratings of OCD symptoms were completed at pre- and posttreatment and follow-up. Length of treatment, number of sessions, and length of follow-up period varied across children. On average, children attended 10.44 sessions over an 8-month period with follow-up data collected 7.3 months following the completion of treatment. Repeated measures analyses of variance revealed that posttreatment and follow-up ratings were significantly improved when compared with those completed at pretreatment. Six children were described as asymptomatic at posttreatment, and nine were symptom free at the time of follow-up. A strength of this study is the use of a sample size large enough to allow for data to be analyzed using inferential statistical procedures. However, the study contains a number of methodological flaws, including the following: Application of treatment was not standardized across children; identical measures were not completed on all children; treatment effects were confounded by the presence of concurrent therapies; and no control group was used. Replication studies that control for these confounding variables are necessary to provide conclusive evidence for the efficacy of the manualized treatment package.

In summary, it is clear that definitive conclusions about the efficacy of psychotherapeutic treatments for childhood OCD cannot be made at this time. However, there is strong empirical evidence for E/RP as the treatment of choice for adults with OCD and preliminary support regarding the efficacy of this approach for childhood OCD. In addition, our clinical experience suggests that E/RP is a highly effective treatment for children and adolescents with OCD. Thus, it is recommended that clinicians apply E/RP as the primary psychotherapeutic intervention for childhood OCD while research efforts continue to focus on providing conclusive evidence regarding the efficacy of this treatment approach for use with this population. A detailed description of the use of E/RP to treat youth with OCD is provided below.

E/RP: Theoretical Underpinnings

E/RP entails subjecting an individual to a feared object or situation and blocking rituals or avoidance behavior until anxiety is reduced. Habituation and extinction are believed to be the factors responsible for the effectiveness of E/RP. Habituation is the process by which the strength of one's response to a particular stimulus decreases over time if the stimulus is presented repeatedly or for a prolonged period (Zimbardo, 1985). For example, decreases in heart rate and subjective anxiety have been reported in adults with OCD after they were exposed to an anxiety-arousing situation for a prolonged period of time (see Beck & Bourg, 1993; Stanley, 1992). Likewise, if children were to remain in a situation that initially aroused high levels of anxiety, their anxiety would be expected to attenuate over time due to the natural process of habituation.

Learning theory goes on to explain symptom reduction in terms of an extinction paradigm that involves disruption of the negative reinforcement loop that is believed to perpetuate obsessive-compulsive symptoms. Wolpe (1990) defines negative reinforcement as the process of increasing the strength of a response by contingent removal of an aversive condition. In the case of OCD, negative reinforcement occurs when a child experiences relief from anxiety (the aversive condition) after performing a ritual and, thus, is more likely to perform the ritual in the future. For example, the child with contamination fears will continue to engage in handwashing rituals because he or she has inadvertently learned that doing so will reduce or eliminate feelings of anxiety. The use of response prevention interferes with the association between ritualistic behavior and anxiety reduction by stopping the child from performing rituals, thus providing the opportunity for anxiety to decrease through habituation. When anxiety reduction is no longer perceived as contingent on performance of ritualistic behaviors, the display of such behaviors is eliminated through the process of extinction.

E/RP: Treatment Implementation

There are a number of variations in the manner in which E/RP can be administered. Exposure can be performed in a graded fashion or through flooding. Graded exposure involves constructing a hierarchy of anxiety-provoking stimuli and then exposing the child to the stimuli in a sequential manner. To develop the hierarchy, the therapist elicits information from the child and parents to generate a list of situations that produce anxiety. Each item on the list is rated by the child using a developmentally appropriate SUDS scale, and then items are placed in a hierarchy from least to most anxiety provoking. At each step along the hierarchy, the child remains in the presence of the stimulus until such time as his or her anxiety level is reduced. Flooding does not use a hierarchy but, rather, involves prolonged exposure to the most anxiety-provoking stimuli at the onset of treatment. This intense exposure continues until reduction of the child's anxiety level is achieved.

Differences in the application of graded exposure and flooding can be seen in the following case example. John was a 13-year-old boy who presented with contamination obsessions and avoidance of contact with objects that he considered unclean. He avoided touching doorknobs and bathroom fixtures with his bare hands. He would touch bathroom fixtures only after wrapping his hands in many layers of toilet paper, and he covered his hand with his shirt sleeve when touching doorknobs. Furthermore, John refused to use public restrooms. Using a graded exposure approach, the therapist first would involve John in constructing a hierarchy. From least to most anxiety-provoking, examples from John's hierarchy might include the following: (a) touching the doorknob on his bedroom door with his bare hand after the knob had just been cleaned, (b) touching the doorknob on the front door of his school with his bare hands, (c) touching the bathroom fixtures in his home with his bare hands, (d) entering a public restroom without touching anything, (e) using a public restroom and touching the fixtures with his bare hands. Treatment would begin by having John repeatedly touch his bedroom doorknob until his anxiety decreased to a comfortable level. Once John could touch his bedroom doorknob without anxiety, he would be exposed to the remaining items on the hierarchy in a sequential fashion. The pace of the progression through the hierarchy would be dictated by John's anxiety level. For example, he might be able to move through a number of items on the hierarchy during one session if his anxiety level declines rapidly, or it might take several sessions for John to habituate to a single item.

In contrast, a flooding approach would entail prolonged exposure to the most anxiety-provoking stimuli until anxiety diminished. John would be required to enter a public restroom and touch fixtures with his bare hands. He would remain in the bathroom engaged in these activities until he reported that his anxiety subsided, regardless of how long this might take. Discontinuation of an exposure session before anxiety attenuates would be contraindicated, regardless of whether exposure was conducted gradually or by flooding, because this would reinforce John's perception that his anxiety level decreases only when he escapes from anxiety-provoking situations.

Exposure can be conducted using in vivo or imaginal procedures. In vivo procedures, such as those described above, involve exposure to the actual stimuli as encountered in one's environment. When in vivo exposure is not possible or when anxiety levels in the presence of the actual stimuli are unable to be tolerated, the child can be asked to imagine anxiety-provoking situations in lieu of direct exposure. For example, imaginal exposure is indicated in the case of a child with obsessive thoughts about killing a parent. Imaginal procedures also can be used prior to or in combination with in vivo exposure (e.g., having John imagine himself in a public restroom before requiring him to place himself in that situation).

When using imaginal exposure, it is important to elicit vivid imagery by incorporating behavioral, sensory, cognitive, and affective cues into the description of the anxiety-provoking scene. The following excerpt from an imaginal exposure scene for John exemplifies how one can accomplish this:

> Close your eyes and pretend that you're standing in front of the door to the boys' bathroom at school. Nobody is around, and you realize that you will have to open the door yourself. Your heart begins to race and your chest feels tight. You put your bare hand on the doorknob and immediately notice that it feels slimy. You think about all of the kids who have touched the knob with their filthy hands and begin to feel queasy. You really have to go to the bathroom, so you push open the door to enter the room. The smell of urine is overwhelming. You feel disgusted as you look around and see the graffiti-covered lime green tiles above the urinal.

Clearly, the therapist must derive the specific cues that are used in the imaginal exposure scene from information provided by the child. More-over, it is helpful to incorporate the child's actual terminology (e.g., "slimy," "chest feels tight") into the description of the scene to enhance the quality of the imagery.

As with exposure, there are a variety of ways to implement response prevention. Although the ultimate goal of response prevention is to eliminate all rituals, it is sometimes necessary to work toward this goal in a gradual manner. When a child is unwilling or unable to tolerate the anxiety associated with termination of all ritualistic behavior, an intermediate goal of treatment may be to reduce the frequency or delay the performance of rituals. For example, an adolescent who checks to make sure that the front door of her home is locked 30 times before going to bed may be required initially to reduce the frequency of checking behavior by 50% before being expected to stop this behavior entirely. A child who thoroughly cleans his room immediately after anyone enters it may be given a 10-minute cleaning period before bedtime and be instructed to delay any urges to clean until that time. Similarly, scheduling a specific time for engaging in rituals may be used to delay mental rituals (e.g., counting). Although it often is more difficult to prevent mental rituals, given their covert nature, thought stopping is a technique that can be used to interrupt them. This procedure involves instructing the child to yell, "Stop!" loudly in an attempt to disrupt rituals whenever they occur. Over time, the child typically is directed to engage in thought stopping covertly by thinking the word *stop*, or visualizing a stop sign rather than yelling aloud. Once the mental ritual is interrupted, the child can be instructed to delay further ritualizing to a later time, as described above. It is important to keep in mind that complete elimination of rituals is the eventual goal of treatment, because this has been found to be more effective than mere reduction or delay of ritualistic behavior (Steketee, 1993).

E/RP may be administered by various individuals, including therapists, parents, teachers, or the youngsters themselves. Typically, the therapist directs the initial E/RP sessions to model the manner in which the treatment should be conducted and to ensure that the child is able to understand and perform E/RP exercises. After the child has experienced success with therapist-directed E/RP, homework is usually assigned in which the child is expected to practice E/RP outside of the context of therapy. Often, homework assignments are performed under the supervision of parents or teachers who have been trained by the therapist in the administration of E/RP procedures. However, youth who are highly motivated, compliant, and sufficiently independent may be able to complete practice sessions without adult supervision. All homework assignments must be monitored routinely by the therapist to assess compliance with and correctness of the E/RP procedures.

PSYCHOPHARMACOLOGIC TREATMENT

Pharmacotherapy for childhood OCD involves medications that influence the neurotransmitter system. Specifically, these medications inhibit the reuptake of serotonin, resulting in functionally increased levels of available serotonin (Viesselman, Yaylayan, Weller, & Weller, 1993). The serotonin reuptake inhibitors (SRI) typically used to treat childhood OCD in the United States include clomipramine (Anafranil), fluoxetine (Prozac), sertraline (Zoloft), and paroxetine (Paxil). Clomipramine (CMI) has a broad spectrum effect on the neurotransmitter system in that it influences serotonin along with acetylcholine and norepinephrine. In contrast, fluoxetine, sertraline, and paroxetine specifically influence serotonin and are known as selective serotonin reuptake inhibitors (SSRI). CMI is the only medication that currently is approved by the Food and Drug Administration (FDA) for the treatment of childhood OCD.

The most thoroughly studied medication for childhood OCD at this time is CMI (for a review see Allen, Leonard, & Swedo, 1995). Two placebo-controlled double-blind studies have demonstrated the superiority of CMI over placebo (DeVeaugh-Geiss et al., 1992; Flament et al., 1985). Flament et al. (1985) studied 19 children (average age of 14.5 years) with primary OCD. The average length of symptom duration for the sample was 4 years. No formal behavior therapy was conducted during the study period; however, parents were instructed not to participate in rituals, and those children treated on the inpatient unit were required to participate in milieu activities. The study included a 1-week baseline assessment phase followed by 5 weeks each of placebo and CMI in a randomized order. The average daily dose of CMI was 141 milligrams. Assessments included self-report and clinician ratings of symptoms. Results indicated that CMI was superior to placebo in decreasing self-reported and clinician-reported symptoms of OCD. Psychiatrist ratings of recovery following CMI treatment indicated that 74% of the sample were at least moderately improved, whereas only 16% were described as unchanged or slightly improved. However, a number of anticholinergic side effects (e.g., tremor, dry mouth, dizziness, and constipation) were reported among children treated with CMI.

Results of a more recent multicenter study provided additional support for the efficacy of CMI in treating childhood OCD. DeVeaugh-Geiss et al. (1992) studied 54 youngsters between the ages of 10 and 17 years with a primary diagnosis of OCD and symptoms of at least 1-year duration. No concomitant behavior therapy was conducted during the study period. Following an initial 2-week placebo phase, children were assigned randomly to 8 weeks of CMI or placebo. CMI was administered up to a maximum daily dose of 3 milligrams per kilogram or 200 milligrams, whichever was less. Assessments included primarily clinician ratings of symptoms. Results indicated that 60% of those treated with CMI were rated as "very much or much improved" compared with less than 17% of those who received placebo. In addition, greater reductions in scores on symptom measures were noted for those treated with CMI compared with those who received a placebo. Although use of CMI resulted in significant reductions in obsessive-compulsive symptoms, the majority of youngsters who received this treatment also reported anticholinergic side effects.

The specific efficacy of CMI compared with other tricyclic antidepressant medications for the treatment of childhood OCD has been the subject of two studies (Leonard, Swedo, Rapoport, Coffey, & Cheslow, 1988; Leonard et al., 1991). Leonard et al. (1988) conducted a double-blind crossover comparison of CMI and desipramine (DMI; a tricyclic antidepressant medication believed to have no specific antiobsessional effect). Twenty-five children and adolescents between the ages of 8 and 19 years were assigned randomly to two consecutive 5-week periods of CMI or DMI following a 2-week single-blind placebo phase. Dosages of CMI and DMI were increased to 3 milligrams per kilogram, as tolerated. Weekly assessments of obsessive-compulsive symptoms were obtained. Results indicated significantly improved functioning with CMI compared with DMI by the third week of treatment. Furthermore, relapse of symptoms was noted when DMI followed CMI.

Leonard et al. (1991) also evaluated the use of DMI substitution during long-term treatment with CMI for youth with OCD. Twenty-six youngsters with OCD received CMI for 3 months. Half of the sample then had DMI substituted without their knowledge, whereas the other half continued on CMI for 2 months. Finally, all participants received CMI for the final 3 months of the study period. Results indicated that 89% of the substituted group relapsed compared with only 11% of the nonsubstituted group during the 2-month comparison period. Relapsed patients in the substituted group all regained previous levels of improvement within 1 month of restarting CMI. The authors noted, however, that total resolution of obsessive-compulsive symptoms did not occur even with long-term CMI treatment.

Fluoxetine treatment of childhood OCD also has been the subject of a small number of studies (Como & Kurlan, 1991; Geller, Biederman, Reed, Spencer, & Wilens, 1995; Riddle et al., 1992). The only double-blind placebo-controlled study was conducted by Riddle et al. (1992). In this study, 13 children and adolescents with OCD first were assigned randomly to 8 weeks of placebo or fluoxetine and then were switched to 12 weeks of the other treatment condition. Of the 13 children, 11 completed the first 8-week period of the study. No behavior therapy was conducted during the study period. Clinician and self-report ratings of symptoms were obtained every 4 weeks. Within-group comparisons during the first 8 weeks of the study demonstrated significant improvements in clinician-rated and self-reported OCD symptoms for children taking fluoxetine but not for those taking placebo. However, when between-group comparisons were made using change scores over the 8-week period, few differences were noted. Specifically, compared with those in the placebo group, children receiving medication improved on a clinician global improvement measure but not on clinician ratings or self-report measures of OCD symptoms. Due to the significant attrition that occurred during the crossover phase of the study, it was not possible to conduct statistical analyses of that data. However, it is noteworthy that half of the children who switched from fluoxetine to placebo dropped out of the study due to worsening of their symptoms.

Some concerns have been raised regarding the potential for adverse side effects associated with the use of fluoxetine. Riddle et al. (1990) found that half of their sample of children and adolescents treated with fluoxetine developed two or more behavioral side effects that persisted for more than 2 weeks. These included motor restlessness, sleep disturbance, social disinhibition, and a subjective sense of excitation. The side effects were not found to be related to dosage or duration of treatment. However, the side effects resolved once the medication dosage was decreased. These investigators also examined the emergence of self-destructive behavior in 41 youth treated with fluoxetine for OCD and a variety of other disorders (King et al., 1991). They found six cases of youngsters who displayed self-injurious behaviors (i.e., suicide attempts, persistent suicidal ideation, violent nightmares or ideation, head banging) during the course of treatment with fluoxetine. However, they noted that half of these children had a history of self-injurious behavior that predated the onset of treatment with fluoxetine.

The combination of CMI and fluoxetine to treat OCD in adolescents was reported by Simeon, Thatte, and Wiggens (1990). The treatment of six adolescents with moderate to severe OCD was described. All youngsters initially were treated for an average of 17.5 weeks with CMI alone at an average daily dose of 92 milligrams. Fluoxetine was added when it was determined that sufficient progress was not being made with CMI or when anticholinergic side effects were perceived as intolerable by the patients. The addition of fluoxetine (20-60 milligrams per day) reportedly resulted in moderate to marked improvement for all patients and allowed for CMI dosages to be decreased to 25 to 50 milligrams per day. In addition, fewer and less severe side effects were noted with the combination treatment compared with CMI alone. Of note, relapse was reported after discontinuation of medication treatment for four of the six patients.

In summary, the literature contains several well-designed studies that provide support for the efficacy of CMI in treating childhood OCD. Unfortunately, children and adolescents may find it difficult to tolerate the anticholinergic side effects commonly associated with this treatment. Fewer adverse physiological side effects are likely to result from treatment with SSRIs (Viesselman et al., 1993). Although there is preliminary evidence to suggest that fluoxetine may be an effective treatment for childhood OCD, no studies evaluating the efficacy of sertraline or paroxetine have been published to date. Additional double-blind placebo-controlled studies are needed to establish the utility of the SSRIs in the treatment of children and adolescents with OCD.

The efficacy of medication treatments has been studied more extensively in adults with OCD (see Steketee, 1993). It has been reported that medication is not as effective as E/RP in treating obsessive-compulsive symptomatology. In addition, medication side effects often occur, and symptom relapse has been associated with the discontinuation of drug treatments. As such, pharmacologic intervention typically is not recommended as a first-line treatment for adults with OCD. However, when patients are unable or unwilling to participate in behavioral treatment due to intense levels of anxiety and/or depression, medication should be considered as a first-line intervention. The use of adjunctive pharmacotherapy also is recommended for patients who do not respond rapidly or completely to behavior therapy. Given that similar disadvantages have been associated with medication treatments for youth and adults (i.e., side effects, relapse with drug withdrawal), it is recommended that these guidelines regarding the use of pharmacotherapy with adults also be applied to children and adolescents (March, 1995).

PSYCHOSURGERY

Historically, OCD was viewed as an intractable disorder that was unresponsive to psychotherapeutic intervention. Indeed, before recent advances were made in behavioral and pharmacologic treatments, the prognosis for those afflicted with OCD was grim. Given the absence of effective treatment alternatives, invasive medical procedures were sometimes used to treat OCD (Rapoport, 1989).

The efficacy of psychosurgical treatments for OCD in adults has been reviewed by Ibor and Alino (1977) and Steketee (1993). Leukotomy, anterior capsulotomy, and cingulotomy are surgical procedures that entail lesioning areas of the brain thought to be involved in the etiology of OCD. Of note, only cingulotomy is performed in the United States at this time. Rates of improvement in response to psychosurgery vary widely, from 25% to 84%. However, suicide following surgery has been reported for some patients.

Very little information is available as to the use of psychosurgery to treat youth with OCD. Ibor and Alino (1977) found that 29 of 57 patients with OCD who underwent anterior capsulotomy in Europe between 1966 and 1974 had developed symptoms before the age of 20. Five of the 57 patients actually had surgery between the ages of 16 and 20 years and were reported to be substantially improved following the procedure. Levin and Duchowny (1991) described the use of cingulotomy to treat an 11-year-old girl with epilepsy and OCD. The youngster had developed seizures as a toddler and OCD by the age of eight. Her OCD symptoms included checking, washing, and reassurance-seeking rituals. Treatment involved a right anterior cingulotomy, which reportedly resulted in significant improvement in OCD symptoms and elimination of seizures. Clearly, there is not adequate empirical data to support the use of invasive surgical procedures to treat childhood OCD. For both adults and children, psychosurgery should be a treatment of last resort, which is reserved for those with debilitating symptoms that have failed to respond to aggressive behavioral and psychopharmacologic interventions (Steketee, 1993).

SPECIAL ISSUES IN THE TREATMENT
OF CHILDREN AND ADOLESCENTS

Developmental Considerations

Flexibility is required during the assessment and treatment of children and adolescents with OCD to accommodate their varying developmental levels. As pointed out in chapter 2, it is important to use developmentally appropriate language and concepts when assessing children and adolescents. The need for sensitivity to developmental issues is equally important when treating youth with OCD. A number of modifications may be required to explain the treatment rationale to youngsters beginning E/RP in a manner that they can comprehend. March et al. (1994) suggest using a story metaphor to facilitate children's understanding of the treatment process and to help motivate them to participate actively. Using this approach, the child is encouraged to give OCD a "bad name" and to ally with the therapist and parents to "boss back" or "say no" to OCD. The child then acts out the story of "How I Ran OCD Off My Land,"© which describes how the child and his or her allies are able to defeat the enemy (i.e., OCD) and regain control of the child's life (see Appendix C for a more detailed account of this treatment protocol). The use of analogies also may be useful when explaining specific requirements of E/RP treatment. In his children's book about OCD, titled *The Secret Problem,* Wever (1994) describes the special training needed to fight OCD in the following manner:

> This special training is called behavior therapy. The more you train the easier it is to fight the OCD so that it ends up not worrying you at all or only a little. It is like training for a long distance running race. The first training run is pretty hard but it ends up getting easier the more you train. Yet training is hard work. In running you get tired and sore. In OCD training you often feel worried or bad inside. But don't give up; as you train more the worry and bad feelings inside get less and less and you end up beating the OCD. (p. 12)

Just as the explanation of the treatment rationale may need to be altered, the implementation of E/RP may require modification for youth. Children and adolescents may not be able to tolerate the intense levels of anxiety that are associated with the flooding approach to E/RP. Moreover, there are ethical questions about whether or not young children can truly give informed consent to participate in treatments that are likely to produce such significant distress. Thus, graded approaches are recommended for this population. When explaining the process of graded exposure, children may benefit from a visual aid when describing the use of a hierarchy. Often, we will draw a picture of a ladder to illustrate how the child will progress along the hierarchy. It is explained that "when you're standing at the bottom of the ladder, it may seem like you will never be able to reach your goal at the top. If you take one small step at a time, though, you eventually can reach the top." Finally, the therapist must be flexible in the creation of the hierarchy. For example, the initial hierarchy items for a young child with contamination fears may be to draw a picture of germs or read a story about visiting a hospital. Once the child habituates to these items, the therapist can incorporate more traditional methods of exposure into the hierarchy.

Sensitivity to differences between children and adults also is necessary when pharmacotherapy is the treatment of choice. It is strongly recommended that therapists work closely with psychiatrists who are trained specifically to treat children and adolescents. Our experience has been that many parents are reluctant to consider the use of medication for fear that their child will become addicted and need to use it forever. Children also may have the perception that these medications are drugs and that they are supposed to "just say no" to drugs. It can be particularly difficult to allay parental anxiety regarding use of medication if the treatment of choice is not FDA-approved for use with children. Clearly, it takes a skilled psychiatrist to explain the use of pharmacotherapy to children and their parents in order to alleviate these kinds of concerns.

Given that numerous developmental tasks of childhood can be disrupted by obsessive-compulsive symptomatology, the degree to which long-term functioning is impaired may be greater in youth than in adults, who already have mastered these tasks. For example, childhood is the time when individuals learn the interpersonal skills needed to initiate and maintain peer relationships. Increasing independence from parents and a sense of self-sufficiency typically occur during adolescence. The child or adolescent with long-standing OCD symptoms may fail to accomplish these developmental tasks. Thus, after the successful treatment of obsessive-compulsive symptoms, further intervention may be warranted to remediate any skill deficits that remain. For example, social skills, communication skills, or assertiveness training can assist youth to improve interpersonal skills that might enable them to resume a normal developmental trajectory.

Systems Issues

Successful treatment of youngsters with OCD invariably requires the therapist to involve various systems of which the child is a part. Most commonly, these systems include the family and the school (e.g.,

Lenane, 1991). As noted in chapter 2, it is important to collect assessment information from a variety of informants across different settings. In addition, maintenance and generalization of treatment gains can be facilitated by application of E/RP within the context of home and school environments. Although parents are most often involved in supervising E/RP homework, there are some circumstances in which it may be more appropriate to involve school personnel (e.g., Parker & Stewart, 1994). For example, some children with OCD exhibit symptoms primarily within the context of the classroom or in relation to school tasks (e.g., repeatedly checking the accuracy of assignments, erasing and rewriting homework, ordering objects on their desks). In addition, teachers may be relied on to carry out E/RP when parents are unable to perform these tasks consistently within the home setting. This most often occurs when parents are overwhelmed with carrying out other aspects of the treatment, when parental psychopathology is present, or when parents have poor child management skills.

Parents may need intensive training in operant techniques, such as the child management strategies developed by Forehand and McMahon (1981), before they will be able to implement E/RP. Operant techniques consist of strategies in which positive and negative consequences are delivered or withheld contingent on the child's behavior in order to shape behavior in a desired direction. This is important particularly in cases where the child generally is noncompliant with parental requests, because improvement in the child's overall level of compliance is a prerequisite to successful involvement in treatment for OCD. For example, Dale was a 7-year-old boy with contamination fears and avoidance of "germy" objects. In addition, he demonstrated significant noncompliant and aggressive behaviors that his parents were unable to manage. Treatment initially consisted of intensive parent training in general behavior management techniques, such as the use of positive reinforcement and time-out. After parents learned these techniques and decreases were noted in noncompliant and aggressive behaviors, the therapist attempted to engage Dale in designing and implementing an E/RP treatment program without success. Thus, parents were instructed to use operant strategies to set limits with respect to Dale's avoidance behaviors. For example, they provided him with only one towel per day, required him to use plates and utensils they had chosen, and limited the number of times Dale was permitted to wash his hands. Parents were taught to respond to noncompliance with these expectations in the same manner as they did to oppositional behavior that was not anxiety related.

Operant techniques can also be used to improve compliance with specific aspects of treatment. Parents can be instructed to reinforce participation in treatment and completion of E/RP homework assignments to motivate children who must endure lengthy periods of exposure to situations that create intense anxiety. For example, a young child may earn a sticker each time he touches a "contaminated" object, or an adolescent who completes daily homework assignments may be permitted to borrow the family car for an evening. Parents may also use positive reinforcement to increase the frequency of noncompulsive behaviors. For example, if a child has her toys ordered alphabetically on a shelf, her mother could praise her for throwing them into a toy box haphazardly, thereby increasing the likelihood that the child will exhibit this behavior again in the future.

There are circumstances in which the removal of positive reinforcement can be used to decrease the frequency of a child's compulsive behavior. Often, parents become involved in their child's rituals and thus inadvertently reinforce their occurrence. For example, parents may provide large quantities of soap and shampoo for a child with washing rituals or may assist a child with checking rituals to examine all the doors and windows in the home. Parents most often provide this sort of assistance in a misguided attempt to alleviate the child's anxiety or to help the child to complete rituals quickly so that they can move on to other activities. Successful treatment requires that parents remove themselves from any participation in rituals. This also includes teaching parents not to respond to their child's compulsive reassurance-seeking questions. Although it is common for the frequency of compulsive behaviors to increase initially when parents cease to participate in rituals, these behaviors will eventually extinguish in the absence of reinforcement.

There are other ways in which childhood OCD can affect the family system. A child's OCD symptoms can easily become the focus of the family to the extent that other important issues are avoided or neglected. For example, marital problems may be put aside while the parents unite to help their child only to resurface when the child becomes less symptomatic. Additional marital or family treatment may be indicated in these circumstances, because family dynamics are likely to change when the child is no longer the center of attention.

Fortunately, there are a number of helpful resources for families confronting the challenges associated with childhood OCD. The OC Foundation is an organization dedicated to promoting research, education, and treatment of OCD. The Foundation offers educational materials, a referral network of support groups and treatment providers who specialize in OCD, and newsletters for adults and children. Details regarding how to contact the OC Foundation can be found in Appendix D.

SUMMARY

In this chapter, a summary of the current treatments for childhood OCD was provided. A review of the literature on psychotherapeutic treatments revealed only a small number of studies using experimental designs. Preliminary evidence was found for the efficacy of E/RP treatment; however, further empirical support is necessary before definitive statements regarding the utility of this approach can be made. Given that E/RP was determined to be the psychotherapeutic treatment of choice for childhood OCD, detailed information was provided regarding the implementation of this treatment, including modifications required for use with young children. A review of the literature on psychopharmacologic treatments for childhood OCD yielded support for the effectiveness of serotonergic agents (e.g., CMI, fluoxetine), and psychosurgical procedures were described as an intervention of last resort for those with debilitating symptoms that have failed to respond to less invasive treatments. This chapter concluded with an extensive discussion of special issues that must be considered when treating children and adolescents.

Calvin and **Hobbes**   by **Bill Watterson**

4

CASE EXAMPLES

Throughout this book, brief clinical case examples have been provided
to highlight various aspects of the clinical presentation, assessment, and
treatment of children and adolescents with OCD. In this chapter, two
cases are described in greater detail to illustrate the process of assessment and treatment from start to finish. Case 1 recounts the outpatient
treatment of a child with contamination obsessions and washing/clean-
ing rituals, and Case 2 involves an adolescent with religious obsessions
and repeating rituals who received interventions within inpatient, partial, and outpatient settings. Both cases required a combination of
pharmacotherapy and E/RP procedures.

CASE 1: LYNNE

Lynne was a 10-year-old girl whose biological parents divorced when
she was 4 years of age. Her parents shared joint custody, and Lynne
spent roughly equal amounts of time every week living in each parent's
home. Both parents were remarried and had additional children from
their new relationships. Lynne's mother and father had an amiable
relationship and generally were able to communicate effectively regarding shared parental responsibilities. Lynne attended a fifth-grade classroom in a public elementary school, where she achieved above-average
grades. She was a popular student who was involved in many extracur-
ricular activities, including dance and soccer. Her developmental and
medical history was unremarkable.

History of Presenting Problems

Lynne was referred to the outpatient Anxiety Disorders Clinic after
presenting at the emergency room because of an acute exacerbation of

anxiety, handwashing rituals, and fear of being "invaded by germs." Although Lynne reportedly had engaged in episodic bouts of excessive handwashing beginning in the first grade, symptoms did not begin to interfere significantly with her functioning until the month prior to her emergency evaluation. The psychiatrist in the emergency room described Lynne as depressed, hopeless, and unable to cope with her worsening anxiety symptoms. Although it was determined that Lynne did not require inpatient hospitalization, she was given a prescription for fluoxetine (20 milligrams per day) and was referred for an immediate outpatient evaluation due to the severity of her presenting symptoms.

Initial Assessment

The initial assessment in the Anxiety Disorders Clinic included the 20-item LOI-CV, an unstructured clinical interview, behavioral observations, the CY-BOCS, and the NIMH-OC. Lynne obtained a yes score of 12 and an interference score of 26 on the LOI-CV. Although no normative data are available for children, comparison of Lynne's scores to a normative sample of adolescent girls revealed her yes score to be just over 1 standard deviation above the mean and her interference score to be greater than 2 standard deviations above the mean. The LOI-CV items that Lynne endorsed as being most problematic included the following: (a) feeling like you have to do certain things even though you know you don't really have to, (b) having thoughts and words that keep going over and over in your mind, (c) hating dirt and dirty things, (d) worrying about being clean enough, and (e) being fussy about keeping your hands clean.

Completion of a clinical interview with Lynne and her parents revealed that Lynne had frequent obsessive thoughts about germs and contamination, including an intense fear of contracting AIDS. These obsessions led her to avoid numerous situations that she believed to be unclean and to engage in a variety of ritualistic behaviors designed to prevent contamination (see Table 4.1). Her obsessive-compulsive symptoms negatively affected her daily functioning in that she became extremely reluctant to participate in activities outside of her home (e.g., dance class, restaurants, friends' homes, soccer practice). Further questioning clarified that Lynne's resistance to leaving her home and parents was related specifically to fears of contamination and was not reflective of another comorbid anxiety disorder (e.g., Separation Anxiety, Social Phobia, or Agoraphobia). Her fears of contamination and illness were

TABLE 4.1 Lynne's Avoidance Behaviors and Compulsive Rituals

Situations That Were Avoided	*Compulsive Rituals*
Wearing clothes that had been washed at the laundromat where cigarette smoking was allowed	Handwashing whenever she thought she touched something dirty (up to 15 times per day for 20 minutes each time)
Being in places that appeared dirty or messy	Using excessive amounts of toilet paper for cleaning toilet seats prior to use and for wiping herself
Being near people who appeared strange, dirty, or mean	
Touching objects with blood-colored spots on them	Blinking 100 times each night before bed so that she would not become sick and die during her sleep
Touching things that appeared sticky	
Touching money	Arranging objects on her school desk in a manner believed to ward off germs
Touching newspapers	
Using public bathrooms	Making parents "decontaminate" objects by touching them before she would touch them
Eating food away from home	
	Checking to see if anyone touched her belongings
	Asking for reassurance from her parents

not paranoid or delusional in nature, nor were they representative of Hypochondriasis. Moreover, although Lynne reported periodic feelings of hopelessness and dysphoria secondary to her worsening OCD symptoms and the associated impairment in her social functioning, she did not meet diagnostic criteria for a mood disorder. Other diagnostic screening questions revealed no evidence of a thought disorder, suicidal or homicidal ideation, or a movement disorder.

Behavioral observations were made throughout the evaluation process. After her entrance into the therapy room, Lynne asked her parents to sit in her chair before she sat in it. She appeared nervous and hypervigilant, and she was observed to scan the room constantly while sitting rigidly in her chair to ensure that she did not touch anything. Her hands were noted to be red and chapped. Lynne frequently asked her parents whether they thought items in the office that she had touched were clean (e.g., her chair, the pencil used to fill out her questionnaire). She occasionally asked these questions of the therapist as well.

Based on the information obtained from the clinical interview and behavioral observations, the clinician-rated instruments were completed and the diagnosis of OCD was easily confirmed. A score of 26 was obtained on the CY-BOCS, indicating symptom severity in the moderate to severe range. Similarly, Lynne's score on the NIMH-OC was 10, suggesting severe obsessive-compulsive symptomatology.

Treatment Intervention

Following the initial evaluation, Lynne began outpatient treatment. Because she had just started a trial on fluoxetine 2 weeks before she presented to the Anxiety Disorders Clinic, she was maintained on this medication (20-30 milligrams per day) throughout the course of behavioral treatment. No beneficial effects of the medication were reported prior to the onset of behavior therapy.

During the first therapy session, the rationale for graded E/RP treatment was described to Lynne and her parents. Lynne was told how her fear of germs leads her to engage in rituals. It was explained that, because she feels better for awhile after performing rituals, she has come to believe that she needs to wash her hands to make her worries about germs go away. E/RP was described as a way to help her learn that she can feel better without engaging in rituals. She was informed that this can be accomplished only by having her practice doing the things that make her worry about germs without allowing herself to perform rituals. The concept of habituation was explained as follows:

> When you stay in a situation that makes you feel nervous, you eventually will feel better. It's kind of like when you first get into a swimming pool, and the water feels really cold. You may want to jump out of the pool because you don't think you'll be able to stand it. If you stay in the water, though, you get used to it after awhile, and it eventually begins to feel warmer.

She was told that it is not enough to have people tell her that she doesn't need to do her rituals to feel better but that she needs to practice staying in situations that make her nervous so that she can prove to herself that she will feel better over time. Finally, it was explained that Lynne initially would experience anxiety during E/RP treatment and that this would be an indicator that the treatment was working properly.

Given that Lynne frequently involved her parents in her rituals, the first step in the treatment process was to instruct parents to refrain from participating in them. It was explained to the parents that they were inadvertently reinforcing Lynne's fears by taking part in the rituals (i.e., when Mom complies with a request to "decontaminate" a chair, it suggests that there really might be germs on that chair; if Dad responds to reassurance-seeking questions, she is more likely to ask such questions in the future). The plan to remove parents from Lynne's rituals was greeted with intense anxiety by all. Lynne was tearful, and her parents were very concerned that this would force her to do things that would make her too anxious. It was emphasized that parents were not being asked to stop Lynne from engaging in compulsive behaviors; however, they were not to allow their actions to be governed by her rituals. For example, although parents were instructed not to sit in chairs to decontaminate them, Lynne still had the option to choose whether or not to sit in chairs that she perceived to be contaminated.

The next step was to involve Lynne in creating a hierarchy of anxiety-provoking stimuli. Table 4.2 lists the hierarchy items and their accompanying SUDS ratings on a scale from 0 (completely relaxed) to 10 (completely panic-stricken). Over the course of the next 5 weeks, Lynne was given homework to practice E/RP using the items from her hierarchy. Her first homework assignment was to wear clothing that had been washed at the laundromat where smoking was permitted. She had to wear at least one piece of "contaminated" clothing each day of the week. During weekly therapy sessions, we frequently reviewed the rationale for treatment and discussed what Lynne had learned by performing homework assignments. She reported feeling very anxious before attempting homework tasks and during the first 15 to 30 minutes of exposure. By the fifth week of treatment, Lynne reported having much less anticipatory anxiety, and she often forgot about her worries once involved in other activities (e.g., school, dance class, being with friends). She continued to experience occasional intrusive thoughts (e.g., "there might be germs on me"), but she spontaneously began to counteract these thoughts with positive self-statements (e.g., "I've been wearing this outfit all day and nothing bad has happened"). Given Lynne's positive response to E/RP, the frequency of treatment was titrated to every other week to allow her to continue to progress through her hierarchy with a greater degree of independence from her therapist. By the eighth session, Lynne stated that she no longer believed that she had to worry about germs because she had been able to face her fears and "survive." Although Lynne's symptoms had nearly resolved, therapy was not terminated at this time because she was fearful that her symptoms would resurface if she discontinued treatment. It was determined that she would have three more sessions over the next 3 months to gradually wean her from her dependence on therapy. Her desire to

TABLE 4.2 Lynne's Hierarchy Items and Their Accompanying SUDS Ratings

Hierarchy Item	SUDS Rating
Wearing clothes that are contaminated by cigarette smoke	4
Not being able to call parents to talk about germs	5
Being near people who look strange, dirty, or mean	6
Touching things that have been touched by lots of other people (e.g., doorknobs, light switches)	7
Touching newspapers	7
Allowing your brothers and sisters to touch your belongings	7
Being in places that are dirty or messy	7
Touching money	8
Using no more than 20 sheets of toilet paper when going to the bathroom	9
Touching things that appear to be sticky	9
Touching objects with blood-colored spots on them	10
Going to sleep without doing your blinking ritual	10
Using public bathrooms	10
Eating food prepared by strangers	10
Allowing someone you don't know well to touch your belongings	10

continue to attend therapy sessions when they were no longer needed was framed as yet another "ritual" that she performed to alleviate her anxiety. The primary goal of the monthly sessions was to show Lynne that she could maintain treatment gains in the absence of frequent contact with her therapist. Other issues discussed during the final therapy sessions included how relationships between family members had improved as her symptoms had resolved, how she could obtain attention from her parents for being well instead of being sick, and how she felt about plans to discontinue fluoxetine in the future. In the final session, which occurred 8 months after her initial evaluation in the emergency room, Lynne and her parents were informed that symptoms might resurface in the future at times of increased stress, and Lynne was instructed to practice E/RP immediately should this occur. Lynne and her parents were encouraged to recontact the therapist if OCD symptoms recurred and persisted.

Posttreatment Assessment of Symptoms

At the conclusion of the 11th treatment session, the CY-BOCS and NIMH-OC were completed again. Lynne's score on the CY-BOCS fell within the normal range (total score = 1), and her NIMH-OC score of 2 indicated mild symptoms well within the normal range. Moreover, Lynne no longer met *DSM-IV* diagnostic criteria for OCD. Three months after completion of behavior therapy, fluoxetine was discontinued. A follow-up call 1 month later revealed Lynne to be symptom free.

CASE 2: BERNIE

Bernie was a 15-year-old boy who lived with his biological parents and younger sister. The relationship between his parents was strained, and the parents had separated on multiple occasions in the past. Family history was significant for paternal alcohol abuse and a maternal uncle with OCD. Bernie attended a 10th-grade classroom in a public high school. He was in an honors program and actively participated in team sports. Bernie was popular with peers, but he often chose to spend free time with his parents in an attempt to prevent them from arguing. His developmental and medical history was unremarkable.

History of Presenting Problems

Bernie was admitted to the inpatient psychiatric unit on an emergency basis because he was completely incapacitated by his need to repeat behaviors until they felt "just right," and he expressed a clear desire to kill himself to alleviate his distress. We received a consult from his treatment team on the unit, requesting assistance with diagnosis and treatment recommendations. At the time of admission, Bernie reported a 3-month history of obsessive fears of dying, which caused him to engage in a variety of rituals. Symptoms gradually worsened over time with a marked increase in distress and impairment occurring during the week prior to his hospitalization.

Initial Assessment

The consultation included administration of the card sort version of the LOI-CV, the Beck Depression Inventory (BDI; Beck & Steer, 1987), an unstructured clinical interview, behavioral observations, the CY-BOCS, and the NIMH-OC. Bernie obtained a yes score of 22, a total resistance score of 43, and a total interference score of 40 on the LOI-CV. Compared with a sample of normal adolescents (Berg, Rapoport, & Flament, 1986), Bernie's scores were significantly elevated (yes score greater than 1 standard deviation, total resistance score greater

TABLE 4.3 Bernie's Avoidance Behaviors and Compulsive Rituals

---

Avoiding certain foods that he really liked as a "promise to God" or to make sure that he wouldn't die

Avoiding saying certain things in response to random obsessive thoughts that he would die if he said them

Checking the stove, locks, ashtrays, and his school work

Repeating routine activities (e.g., going in and out of doors, getting up and down from chairs)

Lining up objects in a perfectly symmetrical manner

Hoarding leaves, sticks, rocks, and bits of paper

Reassurance seeking about whether or not it was OK not to perform rituals

Dressing and undressing in a certain order

Touching objects repeatedly until it felt just right

Getting stuck going back and forth between different ways of doing something until he did it "the right way" or the way he thought God wanted him to do it

---

than 4 standard deviations, and total interference score greater than 3 standard deviations above their respective means). Bernie's scores were comparable to those obtained by other adolescents with a diagnosis of OCD. He obtained a score of 17 on the BDI, indicating the presence of mild to moderate depressive symptoms. Although he reported ongoing suicidal ideation, he no longer expressed suicidal intent.

Completion of the clinical interview revealed that Bernie experienced nearly constant obsessions about dying if he did not perform rituals to make amends to God for a broken promise. He engaged in a wide variety of rituals (see Table 4.3) that typically were performed until he felt that they were done just right. At the time of his admission to the hospital, Bernie was engaging in rituals continuously during waking hours and frequently became stuck in his rituals and was unable to move forward with activities. For example, Bernie often got stuck in his bedroom because he repeatedly had to touch certain spots on his floor. Each time he would approach the doorway, he felt the urge to return to another part of the room to touch a spot that he had missed. His parents would have to physically escort him out of the room to terminate the ritual. Although Bernie reported some depressive symptoms during the week prior to his inpatient admission, these occurred in response to his worsening functional impairment, and he did not meet diagnostic criteria for a mood disorder. Other diagnostic screening questions revealed no evidence of any comorbid psychiatric disorders. However, Bernie repeated a variety of motor acts, and it was unclear whether all of these were ritualistic behaviors or whether he also might have a movement disorder (e.g., Chronic Motor Tics).

Behavioral observations provided a wealth of information regarding Bernie's symptom profile. Regardless of when Bernie was observed or what task he was being asked to perform, he engaged in almost constant ritualistic behaviors. For example, the following observations were made during Bernie's walk from his room on the unit to the examination room:

> Bernie was hunched over, and his gait was unsteady as he walked. It took him 20 tries to get through his bedroom door because he kept returning to the room to touch a spot on the baseboard near his dresser. Finally, he burst out of the room quickly but continued to look toward the door, occasionally moving back toward the doorway before making another quick series of steps down the hall. As he moved forward, he repeatedly ran back to touch spots on the floor and baseboards along the hallway. When he reached the doorway to the examination room, Bernie began to do a series of jerky double-stepping movements forward and backward. He stopped suddenly and bent down to pick up a tissue from the floor. He then put it back where he got it and picked it up again several times before eventually placing the tissue in his pocket. When he entered the room, Bernie initially moved toward a chair located on his left. He then noticed another chair on his right and started toward it. This pattern of looking and moving back and forth between the two chairs continued until he was guided by a staff member to sit in one of them.

Given the severity of his symptoms, Bernie was unable to complete self-report measures without special modifications. During administration of the LOI-CV, he became stuck repeatedly while attempting to sort the cards. Thus, the examiner allowed Bernie to give his answers verbally, and she sorted the cards accordingly.

Based on information obtained from the clinical interview and behavioral observations, the clinician-rated instruments were completed, and the diagnosis of OCD was confirmed. A score of 32 was obtained on the CY-BOCS, indicating symptom severity in the severe to extreme range. Bernie's score of 14 on the NIMH-OC suggested very severe symptomatology.

Treatment Intervention

After the consultation was completed, our diagnostic impressions and treatment recommendations were presented to the inpatient clinical team. It was recommended that inpatient staff learn to administer E/RP on the unit and that given the severity of Bernie's symptoms, the child psychiatrist consider the use of medication. A flooding approach to E/RP was suggested due to the pervasive and incapacitating nature of Bernie's symptomatology. The team agreed to these recommendations and requested additional guidance and supervision regarding the development and implementation of an E/RP program. The treatment rationale was explained to Bernie and his parents, and they agreed to participate in E/RP treatment. However, Bernie expressed concern regarding his ability to do E/RP independently because he felt he had no control over his symptoms. He indicated that he needed direction from others to stop ritualizing. Therefore, a plan was developed in which unit staff were instructed to provide constant direction to guide Bernie's activities away from ritualistic behaviors. Staff members had to issue firm, direct commands (e.g., "Stand up. Walk quickly down the middle of the hallway right now. Come directly to me without touching anything.") and provide strict time limits within which he was required to complete routine daily activities (e.g., 5 minutes to get dressed, 10 minutes to shower).

Behavioral treatment started on Bernie's third day in the hospital, and he subsequently began treatment with 20 milligrams of fluoxetine on Day 6. By Day 13, significant improvements were noted. Although Bernie continued to require direction from staff, he got stuck less often, performed tasks more quickly, and walked with improved posture and gait such that he appeared less impaired. He gradually began to direct himself to inhibit rituals and, thus, required less external prompting to perform E/RP. Given these improvements, Bernie was transferred to partial hospitalization, where he was required to spend increasing amounts of time at home prior to his discharge on Day 20. During the partial hospitalization, his parents were taught how to implement E/RP at home in the same manner as performed by the inpatient staff. Bernie initially became more symptomatic after his transition to a less restrictive level of care. However, by the time of discharge, his behavior in the partial hospital program reflected a recovery of previous treatment gains, and these improvements had begun to generalize to the home setting as well.

The discharge plan included weekly outpatient behavior therapy in the Anxiety Disorders Clinic and maintenance on 20 milligrams of fluoxetine per day. In addition, his school department agreed to provide an aide in his regular education public school classroom. The aide was to remain with Bernie throughout the school day and provide verbal prompts to direct him away from ritualistic behaviors. The school also provided Bernie with a word processor to use for written assignments, because he frequently got stuck when attempting to complete paper-and-pencil tasks.

As he transitioned from partial hospitalization to outpatient therapy, Bernie's symptoms again worsened. His parents and the school aide needed to provide constant direction to Bernie to prevent rituals. Within 2 weeks after discharge, his behavior at school had improved significantly, although symptom severity was noted to worsen at times of heightened stress (e.g., the frequency of his religious obsessions increased when the topic of world religions was taught in his social studies class). Despite these gains in the school setting, Bernie continued to require a great deal of supervision and direction at home. He was less compliant with his parents' directions to refrain from rituals, particularly those given by his mother, who primarily was responsible for carrying out the treatment procedures. Bernie's father was supportive of E/RP treatment but rarely was available at home to assist the mother. Bernie's mother often felt guilty about being directive and worried that Bernie's increased anxiety when prevented from engaging in rituals was an indication that she was making him worse rather than better. She was provided with much support and education about OCD and its treatment during this time. The importance of consistency was emphasized, and she was reassured that for Bernie to obtain control over his obsessive-compulsive symptoms, he would need to experience an initial increase in anxiety. Other family systems issues also needed to be addressed within the context of outpatient therapy sessions. Bernie's parents were in the midst of significant marital conflict and were determining whether or not to separate. Bernie stated that his parents would need to remain together to take care of him while he was sick. His parents were encouraged to convey to him that their decision regarding separation would not be based on whether or not Bernie was having difficulties with his OCD.

During individual therapy sessions, Bernie's progress was reviewed, and the need for him to take more responsibility for E/RP practice at home was discussed. He developed a list of things that he could practice daily for E/RP homework, which he kept track of on a self-monitoring form (see Table 4.4). Initial tasks involved setting time limits within which to complete daily activities (e.g., getting dressed, taking showers). Once Bernie demonstrated success with these tasks, he became motivated to build in daily practice of more challenging tasks. For

TABLE 4.4 Bernie's Homework Self-Monitoring Form

Date	Get dressed in the morning in less than 5 minutes	Take a shower in less than 10 minutes	Get dressed for bed in less than 5 minutes	Do homework in less than 2 hours	Brush teeth and wash up at night in less than 3 minutes
Tuesday					
Wednesday					
Thursday					
Friday					
Saturday					
Sunday					
Monday					
Tuesday					

If Bernie is able to get dressed in the mornings in 5 minutes or less 75% of the days, then he will earn time on the computer at the office.
If Bernie is able to get 40 checks, then he will earn Gameboy time at the office.

example, he agreed to practice walking up and down stairs without engaging in touching and stepping rituals. Bernie requested to earn rewards during therapy sessions (i.e., using the computer, playing Gameboy) for successful completion of E/RP homework assignments.

Posttreatment Assessment of Symptoms

At this time, Bernie has completed 4 weeks of outpatient therapy. Self-report data and clinician ratings of the severity of OCD symptomatology have been collected again to monitor treatment effects. On the LOI-CV, Bernie obtained a yes score of 17, a total resistance score of 47, and a total interference score of 30. Thus, the yes score and total interference score were improved compared with pretreatment scores, and Bernie reported an increase in his efforts to resist obsessive-compulsive symptoms. When compared with normative data, Bernie's yes score fell within 1 standard deviation of the mean, his total resistance score remained greater than 4 standard deviations above the mean, and his total interference score fell below 3 standard deviations above the mean. His score of 15 on the BDI continued to indicate mild to moderate depressive symptoms.

Completion of the CY-BOCS yielded a score of 22, which falls within the moderate to severe range of severity. This represents a marked improvement from his previous score of 32 (severe to extreme symptom severity). His score of 9 on the NIMH-OC fell within the clinical obsessive-compulsive behavior range, which is an improvement from his previous score of 14 (very severe obsessive-compulsive behavior). Although these improvements are encouraging, significant functional impairments persist due to his obsessive-compulsive symptoms. Continued behavioral and pharmacological treatments were deemed necessary based on the updated assessment results and are being provided in an attempt to achieve further symptom improvement.

SUMMARY

In this chapter, two detailed case examples were provided to illustrate the process of assessing and treating youngsters with OCD. The first case involved application of graded E/RP on an outpatient basis for the treatment of a child with contamination obsessions and washing/cleaning rituals. This case demonstrated how to explain the treatment rationale using developmentally appropriate language. Strategies for removing parents from participation in rituals and addressing overdependence on therapy were provided. The second case described the use of flooding to treat an adolescent with religious obsessions and repeating rituals across inpatient, partial, and outpatient settings. This case exemplified how OCD symptoms can interfere with the completion of assessment tasks and highlighted the importance of working with various systems (i.e., inpatient staff, parents, school personnel) to implement treatment effectively. In addition, this case illustrated the need to consider the function of the child's OCD symptoms within the family system.

5

FINAL COMMENTS

Throughout this book, we have presented the most up-to-date information regarding childhood OCD based on the available empirical literature and our clinical experience assessing and treating youth with this disorder. Although the empirical study of childhood OCD is in its infancy, the extensive literature on OCD in adults provides guidance regarding potential research directions. This chapter will highlight areas that deserve immediate attention to advance our understanding of this debilitating disorder in children and adolescents.

There is very limited information available regarding the epidemiology of childhood OCD. Studies that have been conducted generally have included only adolescents, and results have varied depending on the sample assessed. Further studies are needed to determine the prevalence, symptom onset, and prognosis of OCD in youth of all ages and of varied racial, ethnic, geographic, and socioeconomic backgrounds. In addition, because the etiology of OCD remains a mystery, more emphasis must be placed on investigating promising biological models that could reveal risk factors for the development of OCD. Knowledge of biological mechanisms that predispose individuals to OCD, in combination with data regarding factors that may precipitate symptom onset in those at risk, would facilitate the formulation of interventions to prevent and treat childhood OCD.

Although a number of instruments are available that can assist clinicians and researchers in diagnosing OCD and assessing symptom severity, additional data regarding psychometric properties in samples of children and adolescents are needed. For example, there are no reliability or validity data on the most commonly used clinician-rated instruments (i.e., NIMH-OC, CY-BOCS), and normative data on the LOI-CV is lacking for children under 13 years old.

Several researchers have begun to evaluate the effectiveness of E/RP with children and adolescents with promising results. However, well-controlled treatment outcome studies are needed using larger samples, improved measurement techniques, and clearly defined treatment protocols. It is likely that multisite collaboration will be necessary to obtain adequate sample sizes to allow for appropriate statistical analyses and generalizability of findings.

The methodology used in psychopharmacologic treatment studies has been much more sophisticated than that used in psychotherapeutic treatment studies to date. Nonetheless, replication studies are required to demonstrate the efficacy of fluoxetine, and research must be conducted on the new SSRIs (e.g., sertraline, fluvoxamine), given that youngsters appear to be able to tolerate these medications better than CMI. Clearly, an eventual goal of the treatment outcome literature should be to compare the efficacy of medication and behavioral treatments and to determine which treatments (alone or in combination) work most effectively for which patients.

A number of other issues should be evaluated in future treatment outcome studies, regardless of the treatments being studied. Given the chronicity of OCD, it is important that longitudinal data be collected to evaluate the long-term efficacy of treatment and to identify factors associated with symptom relapse. Factors unique to the treatment of children and adolescents should also be the subject of future investigation. For example, the ability of parents to use effective behavior management techniques is likely to influence treatment outcome in children given the degree to which parents must be involved in the implementation of E/RP. Similarly, modifications in treatment may be required depending on patient characteristics (e.g., developmental level). For instance, a child's cognitive level may determine whether imaginal procedures will be useful in E/RP, and pubertal status may influence optimal medication dosing.

The empirical evaluation of childhood OCD is a recent undertaking. Given this fact, we find ourselves with more questions than answers at this time. Although much work is left to be done, it is encouraging to see the advances that have been made within the last decade.

APPENDIX A

CHILDREN'S YALE-BROWN
OBSESSIVE COMPULSIVE SCALE (CY-BOCS)

Children's Obsessions Checklist

"x" all that apply. Mark the principal symptoms with a "P".

Current	Past	
		CONTAMINATION OBSESSIONS
☐	☐	Concern with dirt, germs, certain illnesses (e.g., AIDS)
☐	☐	Concerns or disgust with bodily wastes or secretions (e.g., urine, feces, saliva)
☐	☐	Excessive concern with environmental contaminants (e.g., asbestos, radiation, toxic waste)
☐	☐	Excessive concern with household items (e.g., cleaners, solvents)
☐	☐	Excessive concern about animals/insects
		CONTAMINATION OBSESSIONS (Continued)
☐	☐	Excessively bothered by sticky substances or residues
☐	☐	Concerned will get ill because of contaminants
☐	☐	Concerned will get others ill by spreading contaminants (aggressive)
☐	☐	No concern with consequences of contamination other than how it might feel*
☐	☐	Other (Describe):_____
		AGGRESSIVE OBSESSIONS
☐	☐	Fear might harm self
☐	☐	Fear might harm others
☐	☐	Fear harm will come to self
☐	☐	Fear harm will come to others because something child did or did not do
☐	☐	Violent or horrific images
☐	☐	Fear of blurting out obscenities or insults
☐	☐	Fear of doing something else embarrassing
☐	☐	Fear will act on unwanted impulses (e.g., stab a family member)
☐	☐	Fear will steal things

Current	Past	
☐	☐	Fear will be responsible for something else terrible happening (e.g., fire, burglary, flood)
☐	☐	Other (Describe):_____
		HOARDING/SAVING OBSESSIONS
☐	☐	Fear of losing things
		MAGICAL THOUGHTS/SUPERSTITIOUS OBSESSIONS
☐	☐	Lucky/unlucky numbers
☐	☐	Other (Describe):_____
		SOMATIC OBSESSIONS
☐	☐	Excessive concern with illness or diseases *
☐	☐	Excessive concern with body part or aspect of appearance (e.g., dysmorphophobia) *
		RELIGIOUS OBSESSIONS
☐	☐	Excessive concern or fear of offending religious objects (God)
☐	☐	Excessive concern with right/wrong, morality
☐	☐	Other (Describe):_____
		MISCELLANEOUS OBSESSIONS
☐	☐	Need to know or remember
☐	☐	Fear of saying certain things
☐	☐	Fear of not saying just the right thing
☐	☐	Intrusive (nonviolent) images
☐	☐	Intrusive sounds, words, music, or numbers
☐	☐	Other (Describe):_____

Children's Compulsions Checklist

"x" all that apply. Mark the principal symptoms with a "P".

Current	Past	
		WASHING/CLEANING COMPULSIONS
☐	☐	Excessive or ritualized handwashing
☐	☐	Excessive or ritualized showering, bathing, toothbrushing, grooming, or toilet routine
☐	☐	Excessive cleaning of items, such as personal clothes or important objects
☐	☐	Other measures to prevent or remove contact with contaminants
☐	☐	Other (Describe):_____
		CHECKING COMPULSIONS
☐	☐	Checking locks, toys, school books/items, etc.
☐	☐	Checking associated with getting washed, dressed, or undressed
☐	☐	Checking that did not/will not harm others
☐	☐	Checking that did not/will not harm self
☐	☐	Checking that nothing terrible did/will happen
☐	☐	Checking that did not make mistake

Current	Past	
☐	☐	Checking tied to somatic obsessions
☐	☐	Other (Describe):_____
		REPEATING RITUALS
☐	☐	Rereading, erasing, or rewriting
☐	☐	Need to repeat routine activities (e.g., in/out door, up/down from chair)
☐	☐	Other (Describe):_____
		COUNTING COMPULSIONS
☐	☐	Objects, certain numbers, words, etc.
		Describe:_____
		ORDERING/ARRANGING
☐	☐	Need for symmetry or evening up (e.g. lining items up a certain way or arranging personal items in specific patterns)
		Describe:_____
		HOARDING/SAVING COMPULSIONS (distinguish from hobbies and concern with objects of monetary or sentimental value)
☐	☐	Difficulty throwing things away, saving bits of paper, string, etc.
☐	☐	Other (Describe):_____
		EXCESSIVE MAGICAL GAMES/SUPERSTITIOUS BEHAVIORS [Distinguish from age appropriate magical games] (e.g., array of behavior, such as stepping over certain spots on a floor, touching objects/self a certain number of times as a routine game to avoid something bad from happening.)
☐	☐	Describe:_____
		RITUALS INVOLVING OTHER PERSONS
☐	☐	The need to involve another person, usually a parent, in ritual (e.g., asking a parent to repeatedly answer the same questions, making mother perform certain mealtime rituals involving specific utensils.*)
		Describe:_____
		MISCELLANEOUS COMPULSIONS
☐	☐	Mental rituals (other than checking/counting)
☐	☐	Need to tell, ask, confess
☐	☐	Measures (other than checking) to prevent:
☐	☐	harm to self_____
☐	☐	harm to others_____
☐	☐	terrible consequences_____
☐	☐	Ritualized eating behaviors *
☐	☐	Excessive list making *
☐	☐	Need to touch, tap, rub *
☐	☐	Need to do things (e.g., touch or arrange) until it feels just right *
☐	☐	Rituals involving blinking or staring *
☐	☐	Trichotillomania (hair pulling) *
☐	☐	Other self-damaging or self-mutilating behaviors *
☐	☐	Other (Describe):_____

*May or may not be OCD phenomena.

Children's Y-BOCS

---

1. TIME OCCUPIED BY OBSESSIVE THOUGHTS
How much time is occupied by obsessive thoughts?
or
How much time do you spend thinking about these things? How frequently do these thoughts occur?

0	None	
1	Mild	< 1 hr/day or occasional intrusion.
2	Moderate	1-3 hrs/day or frequent intrusion.
3	Severe	> 3 and up to 8 hrs/day or very frequent intrusion.
4	Extreme	> 8 hrs/day or near constant intrusion.

1A. OBSESSION-FREE INTERVAL
On the average, what is the longest number of consecutive waking hours per day that you are completely free of obsessive thoughts?
or
On the average, what is the longest amount of time each day that you are not bothered by the obsessive thoughts?

0	None	
1	Mild	Long symptom-free intervals, more than 8 consecutive hrs/day
2	Moderate	Moderately long symptom-free intervals, more than 3 hours and up to 8 consecutive hrs/day symptom-free.
3	Severe	Brief symptom-free intervals, from 1-3 consecutive hrs/day symptom-free.
4	Extreme	< 1 consecutive hr/day symptom-free.

---

2. INTERFERENCE DUE TO OBSESSIVE THOUGHTS
How much do your obsessive thoughts interfere with your social or work (or role) functioning? Is there anything that you don't do because of them?
or
How much do these thoughts get in the way of school or doing things with friends? Is there anything that you don't do because of them?

0	None	
1	Mild	Slight interference with social or occupational (or school) activities, but overall performance not impaired.
2	Moderate	Definite interference with social or occupational (or school) performance, but still manageable.
3	Severe	Causes substantial impairment in social or occupational (or school) performance.
4	Extreme	Incapacitating.

---

3. DISTRESS ASSOCIATED WITH OBSESSIVE THOUGHTS

How much distress do your obsessive thoughts cause you?

or

How much do these thoughts bother or upset you?

0	None	
1	Mild	Infrequent, and not too disturbing.
2	Moderate	Frequent, disturbing, but still manageable.
3	Severe	Very frequent, very disturbing.
4	Extreme	Near constant and disabling distress/frustration.

4. RESISTANCE AGAINST OBSESSIONS

How much of an effort do you make to resist obsessive thoughts? How often do you try to disregard or turn your attention away from these thoughts as they enter your mind?

or

How hard do you try to stop the thoughts or ignore them?

0	None	Makes an effort to always resist, or symptoms so minimal doesn't need to actively resist.
1	Mild	Tries to resist most of the time.
2	Moderate	Makes some effort to resist.
3	Severe	Yields to all obsessions without attempting to control them, but does so with some reluctance.
4	Extreme	Completely and willingly yields to all obsessions.

5. DEGREE OF CONTROL OVER OBSESSIVE THOUGHTS

How much control do you have over your obsessive thoughts? How successful are you in stopping or diverting your obsessive thinking?

or

When you try to fight the thoughts, can you beat them? How much control do you have over the thoughts?

0	Complete control	
1	Much control	Infrequent, and not too disturbing.
2	Moderate control	Frequent, disturbing, but still manageable.
3	Little control	Very frequent, very disturbing.
4	No control	Near constant and disabling distress/frustration.

6. TIME SPENT PERFORMING COMPULSIVE BEHAVIORS
How much time do you spend performing compulsive behaviors?
or
How much time do you spend doing these things? How much longer than most people does it take to complete your actual daily activities because of the habits? How often do you do these habits?

0	None	
1	Mild	Spends less than 1 hr/day performing compulsions, or occasional performance of compulsive behaviors.
2	Moderate	Spends 1-3 hrs/day performing compulsions, or frequent performance of compulsive behaviors.
3	Severe	Spends more than 3 and up to 8 hrs/day performing compulsions, or very frequent performance of compulsive behaviors.
4	Extreme	Spends more than 8 hrs/day performing compulsions, or near constant performing of compulsive behaviors, too numerous to count.

6A. COMPULSION-FREE INTERVAL
On the average, what is the longest number of consecutive waking hours per day that you are completely free of compulsive behavior?
or
How long can you go without performing compulsive behavior?

0	No symptoms	
1	Mild	Long symptom-free intervals, more than 8 consecutive hrs/day symptom-free.
2	Moderate	Moderately long symptom-free intervals, more than 3 hours and up to 8 consecutive hrs/day symptom-free.
3	Severe	Brief symptom-free intervals, from 1-3 consecutive hrs/day symptom-free.
4	Extreme	Less than 1 consecutive hr/day symptom-free.

7. INTERFERENCE DUE TO COMPULSIVE BEHAVIORS
How much do your compulsive behaviors interfere with your social or work (or role) functioning? Is there anything that you don't do because of the compulsions?
or
How much do these habits get in the way of school or doing things with friends? Is there anything you don't do because of them?

0	None	
1	Mild	Slight interference with social or occupational (or school) activities, but overall performance not impaired.
2	Moderate	Definite interference with social or occupational (or school) performance, but still manageable.
3	Severe	Causes substantial impairment in social or occupational (or school) performance.
4	Extreme	Incapacitating.

8. DISTRESS ASSOCIATED WITH COMPULSIVE BEHAVIOR

How would you feel if prevented from performing your compulsion(s)? How anxious would you become? or How anxious do you get while performing compulsions until you are satisfied they are completed?

or

How would you feel if prevented from carrying out your habits? How upset would you become? or How upset do you get while carrying out your habits until you are satisfied?

0	None	
1	Mild	Only slightly anxious/frustrated if compulsions prevented, or only slight anxiety/frustration during performance of compulsions.
2	Moderate	Reports that anxiety/frustration would mount but remain manageable if compulsions prevented, or that anxiety/frustration increases but remains manageable during performance of compulsions.
3	Severe	Prominent and very disturbing increase in anxiety/frustration if compulsions interrupted, or prominent and very disturbing increase in anxiety/frustration during performance of compulsions.
4	Extreme	Incapacitating anxiety/frustration from any intervention aimed at modifying activity, or incapacitating anxiety/frustration develops during performance of compulsions.

9. RESISTANCE AGAINST COMPULSIONS

How much of an effort do you make to resist the compulsions?

or

How much do you try to fight the habits?

0	None	Makes an effort to always resist or symptoms so minimal doesn't need to actively resist.
1	Mild	Tries to resist most of the time.
2	Moderate	Makes some effort to resist.
3	Severe	Yields to all compulsions without attempting to control them, but does so with some reluctance.
4	Extreme	Completely and willingly yields to all compulsions.

10. DEGREE OF CONTROL OVER COMPULSIVE BEHAVIOR
How strong is the drive to perform the compulsive behavior? How much control do you have
    over the compulsions?
or
How strong is the feeling that you have to carry out the habit(s)? When you try to fight them
    what happens? How much control do you have over the habits?

0	Complete control	
1	Much control	Experience pressure to perform the behavior but usually able to exercise voluntary control over it.
2	Moderate control	Strong pressure to perform behavior, can control it only with difficulty.
3	Little control	Very strong drive to perform behavior, must be carried to completion, can only delay with difficulty.
4	No control	Drive to perform behavior experienced as completely involuntary and overpowering, rarely able to even momentarily delay activity.

10-item Y-BOCS Total (Items 1-10, excluding items 1A and 6A).

APPENDIX B

LEYTON OBSESSIONAL INVENTORY-
CHILD VERSION (LOI-CV)

1. Do you often feel like you have to do certain things even though you know you don't really have to?
2. Do thoughts or words ever keep going over and over in your mind?
3. Do you ever have the idea that your parents or brothers or sisters might have an accident or that something might happen to them?
4. Have you had thoughts or ideas of hurting yourself or people in your family—ideas that come and go without any good reason?
5. Do you have to check things several times?
6. Do you ever have to check water taps or light switches after you have already turned them off?
7. Do you ever have to check doors, cupboards, or windows to make sure that they are really shut?
8. Do you hate dirt and dirty things?
9. Do you ever feel that if something has been used or touched by someone else, it is spoiled for you?
10. Do you dislike touching someone or being touched in any way?
11. Do you feel that sweat or spit is dangerous and can be bad for you or your clothes?
12. Are you worried that pins, bits of hair, or sharp things might be left lying about?
13. Do you worry that things might get broken and leave harmful pieces?
14. Do knives, hatchets, or other dangerous things in your home make you nervous?
15. Do you worry a bit about being clean enough?
16. Are you fussy about keeping your hands clean?

17. Do you ever clean your room or your toys when they are not really dirty in order to make them extra clean?
18. Do you take care that your clothes are always neat and clean whatever you are playing at?
19. Do you have special places where you put your things down?
20. When you put things away at night, do they have to be put away just right?
21. Are you very careful that your room is always neat?
22. Do you get angry if other children mess up your desk?
23. Are you very careful to have neat papers and neat handwriting?
24. Do you ever do papers over just to make sure that they are perfect?
25. Do you spend a lot of extra time checking your homework to make sure that it is just right?
26. Do you like to do things right on time?
27. Do you have to undress or dress in a certain order?
28. Does it bother you if you cannot do your homework at a certain time or in a certain order?
29. Do you ever have to do things over and over a certain number of times before they seem quite right?
30. Do you ever have to count several times or go through numbers in your mind?
31. Do you ever have trouble finishing your school work or chores because you have to do something over and over again?
32. Do you have a favorite or special number that you like to count up to a lot, or do things just that number of times?
33. Do you often have a bad conscience because you've done something no one else thinks is bad?
34. Do you worry a lot if you've done something not exactly the way you like it?
35. Do you always give a poor report in class even when you planned just what to say before?
36. Do you have trouble making up your mind?
37. Do you go over things a lot that you have done because you aren't sure that they were the right thing to do?
38. Do you keep a lot of things around in your room that you really don't need?
39. Is your room crowded with old toys, string, boxes, games, or clothes just because you think they might be needed some day?
40. Do you save up your allowance or money that the family gives you?

41. Do you spend a lot of time counting your allowance and arranging it?
42. Do you have special games you play for "good luck" like not stepping on or near cracks in the street or sidewalk?
43. Do you move or talk in just a special way to avoid bad luck?
44. Do you have special numbers or words to say just because it keeps bad luck or bad things away?

APPENDIX C

"HOW I RAN OCD OFF MY LAND"©
MANUALIZED TREATMENT PROTOCOL

A Guide to Cognitive-Behavioral Psychotherapy for Children and Adolescents With Obsessive-Compulsive Disorder (Excerpted)

John March, M.D., M.P.H. and Karen Mulle, B.S.N., M.T.S.

On the following pages, we present a guide to the cognitive-behavioral treatment of obsessive-compulsive disorder (OCD). Each session includes a statement of goals and a means of evaluating the outcome. The astute reader will notice that topics from the next session are always introduced at the end of the preceding session. For example, trial exposure and response tasks begin almost immediately, but formal exposure and response prevent (E/RP) does not start until the "transition zone" mechanism for negotiating graded exposure has been carefully and clearly co-located and the child has his or her "tool kit" in place. Similarly, we anticipate involving parents at week 6 by rehearsing parental E/RP with the child at week 5. In our experience, scheduling interventions in this fashion dramatically reduces anticipatory anxiety.

In describing the intervention procedures, we move frequently between the third person ("the therapist should...") and the first person ("we often ask...") in order to present instructions both directly and by example. Unless otherwise specified, the term "children" refers to both children and adolescents. Hundreds of child patients and more than 1,000 hours of therapist experience with child and adolescent OCD have gone into this manual. Along the way we have made plenty of mistakes and taken lots of therapeutic detours, most of which you can avoid by following the manual. Children and families react differently to OCD, and OCD varies tremendously in its manifestations; so feel free to improvise when circumstances dictate. Remember though that OCD is the enemy; failure to focus on OCD (for example, by discussing peer or family problems instead of the session goals) makes the therapist an ally of OCD through complicity with antiexposure instructions. In our experience, this is a common problem for inexperienced therapists or therapists used to other traditions, especially play therapy or family therapy. Be sure to stay within a skills-based cognitive-behavioral framework, and you will more often than not keep your child patient cheerfully engaged in treatment until one day he or she (gratefully, no doubt) no longer needs your services.

SESSION 1: A MODEL FOR UNDERSTANDING OCD: INFORMATION GIVING AND GETTING

Goals

1. Establish rapport
2. Provide a neurobehavioral framework
3. Explain treatment process
4. Introduce story metaphors

1. Nuts and Bolts of Treatment

1.1 Establish Rapport. To enlist the child's cooperation in therapy, session 1 begins with small talk designed to establish rapport. In addition, we often ask younger children to choose a game to play at the end of the session. To relieve anxiety, initial questions are focused on the child's background and narrative history. In this way, the therapist notes what interests and strengths the child brings to treatment. Since the child and family are in a battle with OCD, we state at the outset that the goal of treatment is to provide the child with allies and a strategy for "bossing back OCD." Stated differently, the tone and content of the conversation must explicitly and implicitly document that the therapist is on the side of the child and family against OCD. It is often helpful to identify what went well or poorly in previous treatments. (In our experience, blaming the child or parent, an exclusive focus on drug treatment, or failure to consider comorbid conditions, such as depression or an occult learning disability, characterize most treatment failures.) Once rapport is established, the interview focuses on building a common neurobehavioral framework for understanding OCD.

1.2 Provide Neurobehavioral Framework. By reviewing the current scientific understanding of OCD, the therapist places OCD in a neurobehavioral framework: "neuro" as in neurological disorder, "behavioral" as in manifested thoughts, feelings, and behaviors. While we take pains to point out that OCD can be eliminated through actions taken by the child, we also emphasize that OCD is not a "bad habit" that must be corrected. Stated differently, we help the child understand that OCD is a neurological problem that cannot, in any way, be viewed as his or her "fault" or as something the child could stop "if he or she just tried harder." Instead we explicitly present OCD as a "short circuit," "hiccups" or a "volume control" problem in the brain—whatever metaphor the child finds appealing. Using the child's OCD symptoms as a guide to the discussion, the therapist defines a "worry computer" that inappropriately sends fear cues when no threat is present or turns up the volume on fear cues that do not deserve such attention.

In this context, the therapist then carefully defines obsessions as unwanted thoughts, urges, or images that are accompanied by negative feelings. The therapist illustrates these definitions using examples taken from the child's OCD, using obsessive-compulsive symptoms as necessary. Returning to the child's strengths, the therapist then notes that this definition of OCD as "brain hiccups," namely as an illness distinct from the child as a person, leaves the rest of the brain (and child) functioning normally. Analogies to diabetes or arthritis often help to clarify this picture. Finally, using information from the child's prior psychiatric or psychological evaluation, the therapist provides information and answers questions regarding the phenomenology, epidemiology, neurobiology, and appropriate treatment of OCD. For children receiving concurrent pharmacotherapy, the therapist should emphasize the potential synergy of pharmacotherapy and cognitive-behavioral psychotherapy.

By viewing OCD as a specific brain problem, the child can let go of the notion that he or she is the problem, thereby taking a first step toward explicitly defining OCD as the problem and toward giving OCD a name. These related tasks comprise the agenda for session 2, but should be introduced here as part of obtaining a narrative history and building the neurobehavioral framework. Making OCD the problem is the process of linguistically separating OCD as a medical illness from the child (who is thus labeled as an otherwise normal youngster) so that OCD becomes an object in the child's story that can be addressed in treatment. This allows the child, family members, and the therapist to ally against OCD rather than battle with each other over "who is at fault." Naming

OCD involves choosing an epithet for OCD that assists in making OCD the problem by setting up a "good guys" versus "bad guys" dichotomy between the child and OCD. Younger children often choose names like "stupid" or "terrible trouble." Somewhat older children may choose a comic book character or a less than favorite adult. Adolescents usually call OCD by its medical name. Once OCD is clearly identified and named as the problem, the treatment process of "bossing back" OCD begins.

1.3 Explain Treatment Process. "Bossing back" or "saying no" to OCD is the essence of the treatment process. "Bossing back OCD" requires two things: allies and a battle strategy, both of which are virtually always missing when parents and children enter therapy. For the child to be successful in his or her struggle with OCD, we provide allies (therapist, parents, and friends) and strategies (the techniques of cognitive-behavioral psychotherapy). Exposure and response prevention is the core of "bossing" OCD; the therapist serves as "coach" to facilitate the process. In this way, although the therapist controls the structure of the treatment, the initiative is left to the child, thereby avoiding the problem of the therapist telling the child what to do and so missing the mark with respect to E/RP.

It is critical for the therapist to be sure that the child understands the related concepts of E/RP in the context of the statement, "Who's boss, you or OCD?" The exposure principle states that adequate exposure to a feared stimulus will ultimately reduce anxiety. The response prevention principle states that adequate exposure depends on blocking rituals and/or minimizing avoidance behaviors. Exposure therefore requires the child to confront triggers for OCD, for example, holding a "contaminated" door knob. Response prevention takes place when the child refuses to perform the usual anxiety-relieving compulsion, in this case washing hands or using a tissue to grasp the knob. When explaining E/RP, it is always helpful to use examples from the child's OCD to clarify the treatment process. However, you must make it clear that the child will be able to "boss OCD" in the future without any expectation that the child will do so today.

Exposure and response prevention are always threatening for the child, and the implementation or E/RP requires two primary assurances: (1) the child will receive a "tool kit" in the form of coping strategies to use while experiencing anxiety or other dysphoric affects during E/RP; and (2) treatment will proceed at the child's chosen pace, that is, the "allies" will not suddenly become enemies by asking the child to do the impossible. When a child is exposed to a feared cue without performing the usual compulsive response, he or she will invariably experience increased anxiety and, therefore, must be prepared to expect, measure, and tolerate that anxiety. The "tool kit," introduced in session 3, provides this preparation. The therapist sets the pace by coaching the child to choose tasks that he or she is ready to face—usually those that the child has already confronted with some success. By hooking OCD to a different affect, humor also helps alleviate the embarrassment and demoralization children feel as a result of OCD. Since children are frequently secretive about their symptoms, laughing at OCD (not at the child) can help children discuss OCD in a less threatening context, while building their trust in the therapist.

Although the treatment may proceed slowly, there must always be some movement, however small, toward the goal of generating a story in which OCD plays a less prominent part. Otherwise the therapy itself can come to serve as an avoidance behavior. Thus the therapist must emphasize his or her intransigence against OCD on the side of the child and that this shared attitude will not permit the absence of progress.

In this context, the therapist then provides a session-by-session outline of the course of treatment for the child and his or her parents. Introducing stories about other children who have successfully completed treatment is often helpful in making the treatment protocol real to the child.

1.4 Introduce Story Metaphors. The therapist now introduces the idea that the child has a choice about including or excluding OCD from his or her life story. Past chapters have been taken up with OCD; future chapters need not be. Story metaphors are found by selecting out of the totality of the child's experience those aspects (1) that can be readily assembled into an autobiographical or narrative format and (2) that can be used to drive OCD out of the child's life space. Conceptualized in this fashion, children readily incorporate story metaphors into OCD treatment. Story metaphors stimulate the child's hope that he or she can author a more congenial story, namely a story without OCD at its center. As described in session 2, story metaphors are a crucial tool in mapping OCD onto the child's life experience—past, present, and future. In cognitive-behavioral terminology, this map is termed a stimulus hierarchy.

During session 1, the child is asked to write (or dictate) a brief personal story, noting how OCD influences it negatively, but also being mindful that OCD will be "written out" through the treatment process. Anticipating session 2, the therapist suggests that the child choose a disparaging name for OCD. Younger children in particular may wish to write a story about another person or a pet who is a stand-in figure. Careful questioning by the therapist encourages the child to add as much detail as possible. Some children will know right away; others will have to think about it through session 2 or even 3. Since this exercise is primarily aimed at developing a framework for treatment, not history taking, this is acceptable; but the therapist should note that the goal of treatment is for the child to author his or her story in a way that leaves OCD out of the picture. Once OCD is named, the therapist always refers to OCD by this name as a character (and a rather troublesome one!) in the child's story. This both facilitates the process of making OCD the problem and reinforces the story metaphor. The written story is used throughout the treatment process as (1) a motivational tool, (2) a symptom diary for evaluative purposes, and (3) a communicative tool for informing others about the child's progress.

2. Homework

2.1 General Principles. Just as tennis or ballet lessons require practice, a child with OCD must practice "bossing back" OCD in the office and in homework assignments. The therapist must carefully explain these homework assignments to the child, emphasizing the importance of bossing OCD each day, as well as providing reassurance that homework is time limited and specific and, therefore, will be under the child's control. Stated differently, the child must come to understand that he or she will choose only those E/RP tasks that he or she feels quite ready to perform. As explained in sessions 2 and 3, the story metaphor and associated "map" of OCD are the primary sources for homework tasks.

2.2 Homework Assignment. This week's homework assignment is prescriptive. The therapist asks the child to choose a name for OCD and to continue writing (or dictating to a parent) his or her story, using the chosen name for OCD as a character in the story. This naming and story assignment not only serves as a place for the child to tell about specific obsessions and compulsions, but also actively reinforces the concept of making OCD the problem.

3. Evaluations

3.1 Rating Scales. Scales completed as part of the initial psychiatric and psychological evaluation include several copyrighted scales: the Conners Parent and Conners Teacher Rating Scales, Multi-Dimensional Anxiety Scale for Children, Revised Children's Manifest Anxiety Scale, and Children's Depression Inventory. Noncopyrighted baseline rating scales also are obtained during their first visit. These rating scales include the Leyton Obsessional Inventory, Yale-Brown Obsessive-Compulsive Scale, National Institute of Mental Health Global Obsessive-Compulsive Scale, and Clinical Global Impression Scale. The story written by the child will also serve as an evaluative tool throughout treatment. Finally, the Fear Thermometer (introduced in session 2) will be used to assess the child's progress with specific obsessions and compulsions as well as anxiety levels during exposure tasks.

APPENDIX D

RESOURCES FOR
FAMILIES OF CHILDREN WITH OCD

OC Foundation, Inc.
P.O. Box 70
Milford, CT 06460
(203) 878-5669
Info Line: (203) 874-3843
Fax: (203) 874-2826

Anxiety Disorders Association of America
6000 Executive Boulevard
Rockville, MD 20852
(301) 231-9350

REFERENCES

Achenbach, T. M. (1991). *Manual for the Child Behavior Checklist/4-18 and 1991 profile.* Burlington: University of Vermont Department of Psychiatry.

Adams, P. L. (1985). The obsessive child: A therapy update. *American Journal of Psychotherapy, 39,* 301-313.

Allen, A. J., Leonard, H., & Swedo, S. E. (1995). Current knowledge of medications for the treatment of childhood anxiety disorders. *Journal of the American Academy of Child and Adolescent Psychiatry, 34,* 976-986.

Allsopp, M., & Verduyn, C. (1990). Adolescents with obsessive-compulsive disorder: A case note review of consecutive patients referred to a provincial regional adolescent psychiatry unit. *Journal of Adolescence, 13,* 157-169.

American Psychiatric Association. (1994). *Diagnostic and statistical manual of mental disorders* (4th ed.). Washington, DC: Author.

Apter, A., Bernhout, E., & Tyano, S. (1984). Severe obsessive compulsive disorder in adolescence: A report of eight cases. *Journal of Adolescence, 7,* 349-358.

Apter, A., Pauls, D. L., Bleich, A., Zohar, A. H., Kron, S., Ratzoni, G., Dycian, A., Kotler, M., Weizman, A., Gadot, N., & Cohen, D. J. (1993). An epidemiologic study of Gilles de la Tourette's syndrome in Israel. *Archives of General Psychiatry, 50,* 734-738.

Asberg, M., Montgomery, S. A., Perris, C., Schalling, D., & Sedvall, G. (1978). A comprehensive psychopathological rating scale. *Acta Psychiatrica Scandinavica, 271,* 5-27.

Barton, E. J., & Ascione, F. R. (1984). Direct observation. In T. H. Ollendick & M. Hersen (Eds.), *Child behavioral assessment* (pp. 166-194). New York: Pergamon.

Baxter, L. R., Schwartz, J. M., Bergman, K. S., Szuba, M. P., Guze, B. H., Mazziotta, J. C., Alazraki, A., Selin, C. E., Ferng, H., Munford, P., & Phelps, M. E. (1992). Caudate glucose metabolic rate changes with both drug and behavior therapy for obsessive compulsive disorder. *Archives of General Psychiatry, 49,* 681-689.

Beck, A. T., & Steer, K. A. (1987). *The Beck Depression Inventory manual.* New York: Psychological Corporation.

Beck, J. G., & Bourg, W. (1993). Obsessive-compulsive disorder in adults. In R. T. Ammerman & M. Hersen (Eds.), *Handbook of behavior therapy with children and adults: A developmental and longitudinal perspective* (pp. 167-186). Boston: Allyn & Bacon.

Benkelfat, C., Nordahl, T. E., Semple, W. E., King, A. C., Murphy, D. L., & Cohen, R. M. (1990). Local cerebral glucose metabolic rates in obsessive compulsive disorder: Patients treated with clomipramine. *Archives of General Psychiatry, 47,* 840-848.

Berg, C. Z., Rapoport, J. L., & Flament, M. F. (1986). The Leyton Obsessional Inventory-Child Version. *Journal of the American Academy of Child Psychiatry, 25,* 84-91.

Berg, C. Z., Rapoport, J. L., Whitaker, A., Davies, M., Leonard, H., Swedo, S. E., Braiman, S., & Lenane, M. (1989). Childhood obsessive compulsive disorder: A two-year prospective follow-up of a community sample. *Journal of the American Academy of Child and Adolescent Psychiatry, 28,* 528-533.

Berg, C. Z., Whitaker, A., Davies, M., Flament, M. F., & Rapoport, J. L. (1988). The survey form of the Leyton Obsessional Inventory-Child Version: Norms from an epidemiological study. *Journal of the American Academy of Child and Adolescent Psychiatry, 27,* 759-763.

Bolton, D., Collins, S., & Steinberg, D. (1983). The treatment of obsessive-compulsive disorder in adolescence: A report of fifteen cases. *British Journal of Psychiatry, 142,* 456-464.

Bolton, D., & Turner, T. (1984). Obsessive-compulsive neurosis with conduct disorder in adolescence: A report of two cases. *Journal of Child Psychology and Psychiatry, 25,* 133-139.

Clark, D. A., & Bolton, D. (1985a). An investigation of two self-report measures of obsessional phenomena in obsessive-compulsive adolescents: Research note. *Journal of Child Psychology and Psychiatry, 26,* 429-437.

Clark, D. A., & Bolton, D. (1985b). Obsessive-compulsive adolescents and their parents: A psychometric study. *Journal of Child Psychology and Psychiatry, 26,* 267-276.

Como, P. G., & Kurlan, R. (1991). An open-label trial of fluoxetine for obsessive-compulsive disorder in Gilles de la Tourette's syndrome. *Neurology, 41,* 872-874.

Cooper, J. (1970). The Leyton Obsessional Inventory. *Psychological Medicine, 1,* 48-64.

Dalton, P. (1983). Family treatment of an obsessive-compulsive child: A case report. *Family Process, 22,* 99-108.

Desmarais, P., & Lavallee, Y. (1988). Severe obsessive-compulsive syndrome in a 10 year old: A 3 year follow-up. *Canadian Journal of Psychiatry, 33,* 405-408.

DeVeaugh-Geiss, J., Moroz, G., Biederman, J., Cantwell, D., Fontaine, R., Greist, J. J., Reichler, R., Katz, R., & Landau, P. (1992). Clomipramine hydrochloride in childhood and adolescent obsessive-compulsive disorder—A multicenter trial. *Journal of the American Academy of Child and Adolescent Psychiatry, 31,* 45-49.

Fine, S. (1973). Family therapy and a behavioral approach to childhood obsessive-compulsive neurosis. *Archives of General Psychiatry, 28,* 695-697.

Fisman, S. N., & Walsh, L. (1994). Obsessive-compulsive disorder and fear of AIDS contamination in childhood. *Journal of the American Academy of Child and Adolescent Psychiatry, 33,* 349-353.

Flament, M. F., Koby, E., Rapoport, J. L., Berg, C. J., Zahn, T., Cox, C., Denckla, M., & Lenane, M. (1990). Childhood obsessive compulsive disorder: A prospective follow-up study. *Journal of Child Psychology and Psychiatry, 31,* 363-380.

Flament, M. F., Rapoport, J. L., Berg, C. J., Sceery, W., Kilts, C., Mellstrom, B., & Linnoila, M. (1985). Clomipramine treatment of childhood obsessive-compulsive disorder. *Archives of General Psychiatry, 42,* 977-983.

Flament, M. F., Rapoport, J. L., Murphy, D. L., Berg, C. J., & Lake, C. R. (1987). Biochemical changes during clomipramine treatment of childhood obsessive-compulsive disorder. *Archives of General Psychiatry, 44,* 219-225.

Flament, M. F., Whitaker, A., Rapoport, J. L., Davies, M., Berg, C., Kalikow, K., Sceery, W., & Shaffer, D. (1988). Obsessive compulsive disorder in adolescence: An epidemiological study. *Journal of the American Academy of Child and Adolescent Psychiatry, 27,* 764-771.

Forehand, R. L., & McMahon, R. J. (1981). *Helping the noncompliant child: A clinician's guide to parent training.* New York: Guilford.

Francis, G. (1988). Childhood obsessive-compulsive disorder: Extinction of compulsive reassurance seeking. *Journal of Anxiety Disorders, 2,* 361-366.

Friedmann, C. T. H., & Silvers, F. M. (1977). A multimodality approach to inpatient treatment of obsessive-compulsive disorder. *American Journal of Psychotherapy, 31,* 456-465.

Geller, D. A., Biederman, J., Reed, E. D., Spencer, T., & Wilens, T. E. (1995). Similarities in response to fluoxetine in the treatment of children and adolescents with obsessive-compulsive disorder. *Journal of the American Academy of Child and Adolescent Psychiatry, 34,* 36-44.

Goodman, W. K., Price, L. H., Rasmussen, S. A., Mazure, C., Fleischmann, R. L., Hill, C. L., Heninger, G. R., & Charney, D. S. (1989). The Yale-Brown Obsessive Compulsive Scale: I. Development, use, and reliability. *Archives of General Psychiatry, 46,* 1006-1011.

Goodman, W. K., Rasmussen, S. A., Price, L. H., Mazure, C., Rapoport, J. L., Heninger, G. R., & Charney, D. S. (1986). *Children's Yale-Brown Obsessive Compulsive Scale (CY-BOCS).* Unpublished scale.

Grad, L. R., Pelcovitz, D., Olson, M., Matthews, M., & Grad, G. J. (1987). Obsessive-compulsive symptomatology in children with Tourette's syndrome. *Journal of the American Academy of Child and Adolescent Psychiatry, 26,* 69-73.

Green, D. (1980). A behavioral approach to the treatment of obsessional rituals: An adolescent case study. *Journal of Adolescence, 3,* 297-306.

Haley, J. (1977). *Problem-solving therapy.* San Francisco: Jossey-Bass.

Hallam, R. S. (1974). Extinction of ruminations: A case study. *Behavior Therapy, 5,* 565-568.

Hanna, G. L. (1995). Demographic and clinical features of obsessive-compulsive disorder in children and adolescents. *Journal of the American Academy of Child and Adolescent Psychiatry, 34,* 19-27.

Harbin, H. T. (1979). Cure by ordeal: Treatment of an obsessive-compulsive neurotic. *International Journal of Family Therapy, 1,* 324-332.

Hardin, M. T., Epperson, N., Riddle, M. A., Scahill, L., King, R. A., & Ort, S. I. (1991, October). *Children's Yale-Brown Obsessive Compulsive Scale (CY-BOCS): Psychometrics, reliability, and validity.* Paper presented at the 38th annual meeting of the American Academy of Child and Adolescent Psychiatry, San Francisco, CA.

Harris, C. V., & Wiebe, D. J. (1992). An analysis of response prevention and flooding procedures in the treatment of adolescent obsessive compulsive disorder. *Journal of Behavior Therapy and Experimental Psychiatry, 23,* 107-115.

Hodgson, R. J., & Rachman, S. (1977). Obsessional-compulsive complaints. *Behaviour Research and Therapy, 15,* 389-395.

Hollingsworth, C. E., Tanguay, P. E., Grossman, L., & Pabst, P. (1980). Long-term outcome of obsessive-compulsive disorder in childhood. *Journal of the American Academy of Child and Adolescent Psychiatry, 19,* 134-144.

Honjo, S., Hirano, C., Murase, S., Kaneko, T., Sugiyama, T., Ohtaka, K., Aoyama, T., Takei, Y., Inoko, K., & Wakabayashi, S. (1989). Obsessive-compulsive symptoms in childhood and adolescence. *Acta Psychiatrica Scandinavia, 80,* 83-91.

Horne, D. J., McTiernan, G., & Strauss, N. H. M. (1981). A case of severe obsessive-compulsive behavior treated by nurse therapists in an in-patient unit. *Behavioral Psychotherapy, 9,* 46-54.

Ibor, J. J. L., & Alino, J. J. L. (1977). Selection criteria for patients who should undergo psychosurgery. In W. W. Sweet, S. Obrador, & J. G. Martin-Rodriguez (Eds.), *Neurosurgical treatment in psychiatry, pain, and epilepsy* (pp. 151-162). Baltimore, MD: University Park Press.

Insel, T. R., Murphy, D. L., Cohen, R. M., Alterman, I., Kilts, C., & Linnoila, M. (1983). Obsessive-compulsive disorder: A double blind trial of clomipramine and clorgyline. *Archives of General Psychiatry, 40,* 605-612.

Judd, L. L. (1965). Obsessive compulsive neurosis in children. *Archives of General Psychiatry, 12,* 136-143.

Karno, M., Golding, J., Sorensen, S., & Burnam, A. (1988). The epidemiology of obsessive-compulsive disorder in five U.S. communities. *Archives of General Psychiatry, 45,* 1094-1099.

Kearney, C. A., & Silverman, W. K. (1990). Treatment of an adolescent with obsessive-compulsive disorder by alternating response prevention and cognitive therapy: An empirical analysis. *Journal of Behavior Therapy and Experimental Psychiatry, 21,* 39-47.

Kellerman, J. (1981). Hypnosis as an adjunct to thought stopping and covert reinforcement in the treatment of homicidal obsession in a twelve-year-old boy. *International Journal of Clinical and Experimental Hypnosis, 29,* 129-135.

King, R. A., Riddle, M. A., Chappell, P. B., Hardin, M. T., Anderson, G. M., Lombroso, P., & Scahill, L. (1991). Emergence of self-destructive phenomena in children and adolescents during fluoxetine treatment. *Journal of the American Academy of Child and Adolescent Psychiatry, 30,* 179-186.

Last, C. G., Perrin, S., Hersen, M., & Kazdin, A. E. (1992). *DSM-III-R* anxiety disorders in children: Sociodemographic and clinical characteristics. *Journal of the American Academy of Child and Adolescent Psychiatry, 31,* 1070-1076.

Lenane, M. C. (1991). Family therapy for children with obsessive-compulsive disorder. In M. T. Pato & J. Zohar (Eds.), *Current treatments of obsessive-compulsive disorder* (pp. 103-113). Washington, DC: American Psychiatric Press.

Lenane, M. C., Swedo, S. E., Leonard, H., Pauls, D. L., Sceery, W., & Rapoport, J. L. (1990). Psychiatric disorders in first degree relatives of children and adolescents with obsessive compulsive disorder. *Journal of the American Academy of Child and Adolescent Psychiatry, 29,* 407-412.

Leonard, H., Swedo, S., Rapoport, J. L., Coffey, M., & Cheslow, D. (1988). Treatment of childhood obsessive-compulsive disorder with clomipramine and desmethylimipramine: A double-blind crossover comparison. *Psychopharmacology Bulletin, 24,* 93-95.

Leonard, H. L., Goldberger, E. L., Rapoport, J. L., Cheslow, D. L., & Swedo, S. E. (1990). Childhood rituals: Normal development or obsessive-compulsive symptoms? *Journal of the American Academy of Child and Adolescent Psychiatry, 29,* 17-23.

Leonard, H. L., Swedo, S. E., Lenane, M. C., Rettew, D. C., Cheslow, D. L., Hamburger, S. D., & Rapoport, J. L. (1991). A double-blind desipramine substitution during long-term clomipramine treatment in children and adolescents with obsessive-compulsive disorder. *Archives of General Psychiatry, 48,* 922-927.

Levin, B., & Duchowny, M. (1991). Childhood obsessive-compulsive disorder and cingulate epilepsy. *Biological Psychiatry, 30,* 1049-1055.

Lindley, P., Marks, I., Philpott, R., & Snowden, J. (1977). Treatment of obsessive-compulsive neurosis with history of childhood autism. *British Journal of Psychiatry, 130,* 592-597.

March, J. S. (1995). Cognitive-behavioral psychotherapy for children and adolescents with OCD: A review and recommendations for treatment. *Journal of the American Academy of Child and Adolescent Psychiatry, 34,* 7-18.

March, J. S., Leonard, H. L., & Swedo, S. E. (1995). Obsessive-compulsive disorder. In J. S. March (Ed.), *Anxiety disorders in children and adolescents* (pp. 251-275). New York: Guilford.

March, J. S., & Mulle, K. (1995). Manualized cognitive-behavioral psychotherapy for obsessive-compulsive disorder in childhood: A preliminary single case study. *Journal of Anxiety Disorders, 9,* 175-184.

March, J. S., Mulle, K., & Herbel, B. (1994). Behavioral psychotherapy for children and adolescents with obsessive-compulsive disorder: An open trial of a new protocol-driven treatment package. *Journal of the American Academy of Child and Adolescent Psychiatry, 33,* 333-341.

Mills, H. L., Agras, W. S., Barlow, D. H., & Mills, J. R. (1973). Compulsive rituals treated by response prevention. *Archives of General Psychiatry, 28,* 524-529.

Minuchin, S., & Fishman, H. C. (1981). *Family therapy techniques.* Cambridge, MA: Harvard University Press.

Morelli, G. (1983). Adolescent compulsion: A case study involving cognitive-behavioral treatment. *Psychological Reports, 53,* 519-522.

Mowrer, O. H. (1960). *Learning theory and behavior.* New York: John Wiley.

O'Connor, J. J. (1983). Why can't I get hives: Brief strategic therapy with an obsessional child. *Family Process, 22,* 201-209.

Ong, S. B. Y., & Leng, Y. K. (1979). The treatment of an obsessive-compulsive girl in the context of Malaysian Chinese culture. *Australian and New Zealand Journal of Psychiatry, 13,* 255-259.

Ownby, R. L. (1983). A cognitive behavioral intervention for compulsive handwashing with a thirteen-year-old boy. *Psychology in the Schools, 20,* 219-222.

Parker, Z., & Stewart, E. (1994). School consultation and the management of obsessive-compulsive personality in the classroom. *Adolescence, 29,* 563-574.

Pauls, D. L., Raymond, C. L., & Robertson, M. (1991). The genetics of obsessive-compulsive disorder: A review. In J. Zohar, R. Insel, & S. Rasmussen (Eds.), *The psychobiology of obsessive-compulsive disorder* (pp. 89-100). New York: Springer.

Pitman, R. K. (1991). Historical considerations. In J. Zohar, T. Insel, & S. Rasmussen (Eds.), *The psychobiology of obsessive-compulsive disorder* (pp. 1-12). New York: Springer.

Puig-Antich, J., & Chambers, W. (1982). *Schedule for affective disorders and schizophrenia for school-age children.* New York: New York State Psychiatric Institute.

Rachman, S. J. (1985). An overview of clinical and research issues in obsessive-compulsive disorders. In M. Mavissakalian, S. M. Turner, & L. Michelson (Eds.), *Obsessive-compulsive disorders: Psychological and pharmacological treatment* (pp. 1-47). New York: Plenum.

Rapoport, J. L. (1989). *The boy who couldn't stop washing.* New York: E. P. Dutton.

Rapoport, J. L. (1991). Recent advances in obsessive-compulsive disorder. *Neuropsychopharmacology, 5,* 1-10.

Rapoport, J., Elkins, R., & Mikkelsen, E. (1980). A clinical controlled trial of chlorimipramine in adolescents with obsessive-compulsive disorder. *Psychopharmacology Bulletin, 16,* 61-63.

Rapoport, J. L., Swedo, S. E., & Leonard, H. L. (1992). Childhood obsessive compulsive disorder. *Journal of Clinical Psychiatry, 53,* 11-16.

Rasmussen, S. A., & Tsuang, M. T. (1986). Epidemiology and clinical features of obsessive-compulsive disorder. In M. A. Jenike, L. Baer, & W. E. Minichiello (Eds.), *Obsessive-compulsive disorders: Theory and management* (pp. 23-44). Littleton, MA: PSG.

Reeve, E. A., Bernstein, G. A., & Christenson, G. A. (1992). Clinical characteristics and psychiatric comorbidity in children with trichotillomania. *Journal of the American Academy of Child and Adolescent Psychiatry, 31,* 132-138.

Rettew, D. C., Swedo, S. E., Leonard, H. L., Lenane, M. C., & Rapoport, J. L. (1992). Obsessions and compulsions across time in 79 children and adolescents with obsessive-compulsive disorder. *Journal of the American Academy of Child and Adolescent Psychiatry, 31,* 1050-1056.

Riddle, M. A., King, R. A., Hardin, M. T., Scahill, L., Ort, S. I., Chappell, P., Rasmusson, A., & Leckman, J. F. (1990). Behavioral side effects of fluoxetine in children and adolescents. *Journal of Child and Adolescent Psychopharmacology, 1,* 193-198.

Riddle, M. A., Scahill, L., King, R. A., Hardin, M. T., Anderson, G. M., Ort, S. I., Smith, J. C., Leckman, J. F., & Cohen, D. J. (1992). Double-blind, crossover trial of fluoxetine and placebo in children and adolescents with obsessive-compulsive disorder. *Journal of the American Academy of Child and Adolescent Psychiatry, 31,* 1062-1069.

Sallee, R., & Greenawald, J. (1995). Neurobiology. In J. S. March (Ed.), *Anxiety disorders in children and adolescents* (pp. 3-34). New York: Guilford.

Schwab-Stone, M., Fisher, P., Cohen, P., Piacentini, J., Davies, M., Conners, C. K., & Regier, D. (1993). The Diagnostic Interview Schedule for Children—Revised version (DISC-R): I. Preparation, field testing, interrater reliability, and acceptability. *Journal of the American Academy of Child and Adolescent Psychiatry, 32,* 643-650.

Shapiro, E. S. (1984). Self-monitoring procedures. In T. H. Ollendick & M. Hersen (Eds.), *Child behavioral assessment* (pp. 148-165). New York: Pergamon.

Silverman, W. K., & Nelles, W. B. (1988). The anxiety disorders interview schedule for children. *Journal of the American Academy of Child and Adolescent Psychiatry, 27,* 772-778.

Simeon, J. G., Thatte, S., & Wiggens, D. (1990). Treatment of adolescent obsessive-compulsive disorder with a clomipramine-fluoxetine combination. *Psychopharmacology Bulletin, 26,* 285-290.

Stanley, L. (1980). Treatment of ritualistic behaviour in an eight-year-old girl by response prevention: A case report. *Journal of Child Psychology and Psychiatry, 21,* 85-90.

Stanley, M. A. (1992). Obsessive-compulsive disorder. In S. M. Turner, K. S. Calhoun, & H. E. Adams (Eds.), *Handbook of clinical behavior therapy* (pp. 67-86). New York: John Wiley.

Steketee, G. S. (1993). *Treatment of obsessive compulsive disorder.* New York: Guilford.

Steketee, G., & Cleere, L. (1990). Obsessional-compulsive disorders. In A. S. Bellack, M. Hersen, & A. E. Kazdin (Eds.), *International handbook of behavior modification and therapy* (pp. 307-332). New York: Plenum.

Sternberger, L. G., & Burns, G. L. (1990). Maudsley Obsessional-Compulsive Inventory: Obsessions and compulsions in a nonclinical sample. *Behaviour Research and Therapy, 28,* 337-340.

Swedo, S. E., Leonard, H. L., Kruesi, M. J., Rettew, D. C., Listwak, S. J., Berrettini, W., Stipetic, M., Hamburger, S., Gold, P. W., Potter, W. Z., & Rapoport, J. L. (1992). Cerebrospinal fluid neurochemistry in children and adolescents with obsessive-compulsive disorder. *Archives of General Psychiatry, 49,* 29-36.

Swedo, S. E., Leonard, H. L., Rapoport, J. L., Lenane, M. C., Goldberger, E. L., & Cheslow, D. L. (1989). A double-blind comparison of clomipramine and desipramine in the treatment of trichotillomania (hair pulling). *New England Journal of Medicine, 321,* 497-501.

Swedo, S. E., Leonard, H. L., Schapiro, M. B., Casey, B. J., Mannheim, G. B., Lenane, M. C., & Rettew, D. C. (1993). Sydenham's chorea: Physical and psychological symptoms of St. Vitus Dance. *Pediatrics, 91,* 706-713.

Swedo, S. E., Pietrini, P., Leonard, H. L., Schapiro, M. B., Rettew, D. C., Goldberger, E. L., Rapoport, S. I., Rapoport, J. L., & Grady, C. L. (1992). Cerebral glucose metabolism in childhood onset obsessive compulsive disorder—Revisualization during pharmacotherapy. *Archives of General Psychiatry, 49,* 690-694.

Swedo, S. E., Rapoport, J. L., Cheslow, D. L., Leonard, H. L., Ayoub, E. M., Hosier, D. M., & Wald, E. R. (1989). High prevalence of obsessive-compulsive symptoms in patients with Sydenham's chorea. *American Journal of Psychiatry, 146,* 246-249.

Swedo, S. E., Rapoport, J. L., Leonard, H., Lenane, M., & Cheslow, D. (1989). Obsessive compulsive disorder in children and adolescents. *Archives of General Psychiatry, 46,* 335-341.

Thomsen, P. H. (1991). Obsessive-compulsive symptoms in children and adolescents: A phenomenological analysis of 61 Danish cases. *Psychopathology, 24,* 12-18.

Thomsen, P. H. (1993). Obsessive-compulsive disorder in children and adolescents: Self-reported obsessive-compulsive behavior in pupils in Denmark. *Acta Psychiatrica Scandinavia, 88,* 212-217.

Thomsen, P. H., & Mikkelsen, H. U. (1991). Children and adolescents with obsessive-compulsive disorder: The demographic and diagnostic characteristics of 61 Danish patients. *Acta Psychiatrica Scandinavia, 83,* 262-266.

Thomsen, P. H., & Mikkelsen, H. U. (1993). Development of personality disorders in children and adolescents with obsessive-compulsive disorder: A 6- to 22-year follow-up study. *Acta Psychiatrica Scandinavia, 87,* 456-462.

Toro, J., Cervera, M., Osejo, E., & Salamero, M. (1992). Obsessive-compulsive disorder in childhood and adolescence: A clinical study. *Journal of Child Psychology and Psychiatry, 33,* 1025-1037.

Turner, S. M., & Beidel, D. C. (1988). *Treating obsessive-compulsive disorder.* New York: Pergamon.

Viesselman, J. O., Yaylayan, S., Weller, E. B., & Weller, R. A. (1993). Antidysthymic drugs. In J. S. Werry & M. G. Aman (Eds.), *Practitioner's guide to psychoactive drugs for children and adolescents* (pp. 239-268). New York: Plenum.

Wagner, K. D., & Sullivan, M. A. (1991). Fear of AIDS related to the development of obsessive-compulsive disorder in a child. *Journal of the American Academy of Child and Adolescent Psychiatry, 30,* 740-742.

Welner, A., Reich, T., Herjanic, B., & Campbell, W. (1987). Reliability, validity and parent-child agreement studies of the Diagnostic Interview Schedule for Children and Adolescents. *Journal of the American Academy of Child Psychiatry, 26,* 649-653.

Wever, C. (1994). *The secret problem.* Australia: Shrinkwrap Press.

Whitaker, A., Johnson, J., Shaffer, D., Rapoport, J. L., Kalikow, K., Walsh, B. T., Davies, M., Braiman, S., & Dolinsky, A. (1990). Uncommon troubles in young people: Prevalence estimates of selected psychiatric disorders in a nonreferred adolescent population. *Archives of General Psychiatry, 47,* 487-496.

Willmuth, M. E. (1988). Cognitive-behavioral and insight-oriented psychotherapy of an eleven-year-old boy with obsessive-compulsive disorder. *American Journal of Psychotherapy, 42,* 472-478.

Wolff, R., & Rapoport, J. (1988). Behavioral treatment of childhood obsessive-compulsive disorder. *Behavior Modification, 12,* 252-266.

Wolpe, J. (1990). *The practice of behavior therapy* (4th ed.). New York: Pergamon.

Zimbardo, P. G. (1985). *Psychology and life.* Glenview, IL: Scott, Foresman.

Zohar, A. H., Ratzoni, G., Pauls, D. L., Apter, A., Bleich, A., Kron, S., Rappaport, M., Weizman, A., & Cohen, D. J. (1992). An epidemiological study of obsessive-compulsive disorder and related disorders in Israeli adolescents. *Journal of the American Academy of Child and Adolescent Psychiatry, 31,* 1057-1061.

AUTHOR INDEX

SUBJECT INDEX

ABOUT THE AUTHORS

Greta Francis obtained her doctorate in clinical psychology at Virginia Polytechnic Institute and State University. She completed her predoctoral internship and an NIMH postdoctoral fellowship in childhood anxiety disorders at the Western Psychiatric Institute and Clinic in the School of Medicine at the University of Pittsburgh. She is Assistant Professor in the Department of Psychiatry and Human Behavior at the Brown University School of Medicine and Associate Director of the Bradley School at Emma Pendleton Bradley Hospital.

Rod A. Gragg obtained his doctorate in clinical psychology at the University of Kansas. He completed his predoctoral internship and postdoctoral fellowship in clinical child psychology and childhood anxiety disorders in the Clinical Psychology Training Consortium at the Brown University School of Medicine. He is a Clinical Assistant Professor in the Department of Psychiatry and Human Behavior at the Brown University School of Medicine and Clinical Psychologist at the Emma Pendleton Bradley Hospital.